Learning to Spell

A BOOK OF RESOURCES FOR TEACHERS

JOYCE TODD

BASIL BLACKWELL · PUBLISHER

Published by
Basil Blackwell Limited
108 Cowley Road
Oxford OX4 1JF

ISBN 0 631 13197 3 (Cased)
ISBN 0 631 13198 1 (Paper)

Phototypesetting by Oxford Publishing Services
Printed in Great Britain

Contents

Acknowledgements

My grateful thanks are given to all the school teachers, parents and by no means least, the many children who so willingly co-operated in providing the materials for this book.

Joyce Todd, B.A., M.Phil.
1982

On a point of convention, and for linguistic convenience, the author has used *he* to refer to the pupil and *she* to refer to the teacher.

Introduction

Spelling is probably one of the worst taught subjects in our schools today. This is not the teacher's fault; she knows that spelling is a problem area and one of her main pleas is 'tell me how to teach spelling', but there is still very little information available to help her in the classroom situation.

For many years the study of reading has dominated the field of English in the primary school. The teacher is now able to draw upon a vast amount of resources, but when considering the teaching of spelling there is a dearth of information. Why?

Until fairly recently teaching spelling was not considered fashionable. Perhaps more than any other subject it suffered from the belief that learning was 'caught' not 'taught'. Many teachers felt that spelling was associated with 'formal' teaching – with rules and rigid instruction, and, having rejected this style of teaching, they swung to the opposite extreme in the hope that this might provide the answer. However, the teaching of spelling was not so easily avoided.

The Bullock Report (1975) made it quite clear that schools have a responsibility to teach their pupils correct spelling. Peters (1967) also stressed the importance of teaching spelling in *Spelling: Caught or Taught?*, but we are still faced with the problem of how to teach spelling effectively. Many studies have been carried out to devise spelling lists; others have sought to discover what proportion of words are regular or irregular, and attempts have been made to ascertain whether there are common causes which prevent some people learning to spell. However, 'the findings of research studies are not always pertinent to the problems of teachers or of much practical value in the classroom.' (*A Language for Life* p. 552).

This book is written very much with the teacher and learner in mind. However, it is more than just tips for teachers. First it examines the way children learn to spell, and then it describes many classroom activities designed to help in the teaching of spelling.

These activities are based upon the theory that children learn best when they are directing and discovering their learning.

There is also a chapter describing a spelling curriculum for a whole school, and although one quick glance might mislead the reader into thinking it is a nice, easy programme this is far from the truth. The suggested plan relies very much upon the teacher's knowledge and flair for it to succeed, as the author believes that the teacher has the largest part to play in making mere schooling into an educational experience.

In the final section there is a chapter on the remedial situation, for this presents particularly difficult problems for both teacher and learner. The child knows he has failed, and confidence has to be restored before any lasting progress can be made. Also in this final section is a chapter which questions the conventional type of spelling test, and suggests simple improvements.

Finally, there is a chapter addressed to the parent. Parents need to know how they can help their own children and how, inadvertently, they might be hindering the child's progress. It is not suggested that they set up some sort of mini-school, but rather take a supportive role which is perhaps even more important than the amount of knowledge they convey to their child.

There are three pages at the end of the book (pp. 129–131), which are suitable for photocopying by the teacher, and are examples of checklists which may aid her to keep a record of each child's progress.

Spelling, like most other skills, requires a positive attitude on the part of the learner. It is hoped that teachers will absorb, adapt or reject the ideas contained in this book, so that spelling becomes a progressive and inspired activity, not a boring routine to be performed every Friday morning!

PART ONE
LEARNING TO SPELL

1 What is Spelling?

A Definition

Before we can begin to consider how to learn to spell we must first decide what we mean by 'spelling'. It is such a common word that we seldom stop to think what we mean by it, but we require a precise definition in order to clarify what should and what should not be included in a spelling programme. What are the essential ingredients which make up this skill? Just for a moment stop reading and form your own definition of 'spelling'.

Possibly your first attempt is something like this: 'Spelling is knowing how to spell a word'. This will not do. It brings us no nearer to a description of the task. If we consult the Chambers Twentieth Century Dictionary we find the definition given as 'to name or set down in order the letters of' and this would seem a useful starting point. However, to name or set down in order the letters of the alphabet or some fictitious word such as 'xntoeaua' does not constitute spelling in the generally accepted use of the word. We spell *words*.

Thus we have to reproduce, in the correct order, the letters of a word. But this definition is still insufficient, since if we merely copied the letters from a master copy set up in front of us this would not constitute spelling the word, even though all the other ingredients are present.

Spelling involves memory. We must recall the correct order of the letters of a word from memory. Although the time interval is not usually specified, sufficient time must elapse between seeing the word and writing it for the forgetting process to come into effect. In other words, the writer has to demonstrate that he is writing the word from memory. Thus a working definition of spelling is: 'to name or set down from memory, in the correct order, the letters of a word.'

This now seems quite a reasonable working definition. We have a clear aim of what the task is, and in fact the definition makes the task seem quite a simple one. This is one purpose of a definition; to clear the ground of all extraneous matters and get to the heart of the

1

problem. Now let us consider what the task involves – what does spelling look like when performed by both a good and a poor speller?

Good and Poor Spellers

First let us consider two descriptions of the performance of good spellers.

Schonell (1942) likened spelling to a machine-like movement when words
'flow from the end of our pen . . . engram complexes dependent for their stimuli upon dozens of muscles which have been co-ordinated with definite strength, sequence, accuracy and rapidity.' (*Backwardness in the Basic Subjects* p. 277)

Burt (1947) said,
'the type of spelling capacity that is required for practical purposes is the ability to spell words automatically, when the attention is diverted to the purport of the total context, rather than riveted on the orthography of the isolated unit.' *Mental and Scholastic Tests* p. 316)

Such descriptions have never been seriously questioned. We all know that a good speller, when writing, does not attend to each individual letter; the letters follow one another apparently automatically. The writer concentrates upon the task of communicating, unhampered by hesitancy over his spelling.

However, even with a good speller, a 'hitch', as Schonell called it, sometimes occurs. There is hesitancy over writing a word. He may write a few letters and then stop. The habit of immediate recall of each letter has been broken. How does the competent speller overcome this difficulty? He may sub-vocalise the word as an aid to auditory analysis, or he may try out the word a few times to see which feels or looks right. He may consult a dictionary. It is unlikely he will be delayed for long. He soon picks up speed and is off again – writing each word automatically. In contrast, the poor speller may meet a 'hitch' at almost every word; consequently he often writes slowly and hesitantly. He is still at the level of groping for each letter and is therefore unable to express himself freely in writing.

At this point it might be wise to consider what is meant by the term 'poor speller'. We have summarised how a good speller performs, but in practice the performance of a poor speller defies a neat description. All too often those who have difficulties with spelling are assumed to be a homogeneous group, but this is far from true.

2

This passage was dictated to an eight year old good speller. She wrote quickly and competently for the task was well within her capabilities.

> There are seven days in a week and twelve months in a year. Today is Tuesday and the month is February. It is winter but spring will soon be here. Right now we can see some new little green leaves just about ready to come out. Do you know which is the first flower to bloom. What colour is it yellow or white

The degree of difficulty varies considerably. A pupil may make many mistakes but this fact on its own does not make him a poor speller. He may be a careless speller or he may be attempting to write difficult and unusual words. The principal method of identifying a poor speller is by considering whether his misspellings were reasonable or unreasonable alternatives. The following examples are misspellings from good spellers aged 8 years. Although the words were too difficult for them, they all made an attempt and generally the errors were reasonable:

Examples of misspellings of the word 'description'
discription, discrupion, dicription, despictson, discripshion, discriptoin, discripshon

Examples of misspellings of the word 'genuine'
genuin, geuin, genuie, jenuin, jenuwen

Unfortunately, most spelling tests accord a zero score to a pupil if he fails to give a perfect answer, but this dichotomous marking gives little indication of his actual spelling ability. For example, a child gains zero whether he spells 'have' 'hav' or 'hvff', but the first version contains only a slight error and the second suggests a chaotic attempt.

In this book, when reference is made to a poor speller a child who makes errors similar to the second example is assumed, that is, his

3

This passage was dictated to an eight year old poor speller. She was in the same class as the good speller, which illustrates the wide range of abilities found in many classes. The dictation was given slowly and at a pace within her capability. She also had ample opportunity after the dictation to correct any mistakes.

> there are seven 7 in a week
> and 12 mons in a year month
> tooday is teset and the mton
> is febyouer
>
> it is wintet but Spring will
> soon be here
> ritn on we can See Some
> new litte greenlevs Just about
> to came out
> do you no wich is the
> flowe to bloom
> what colu is it yellow
> or white

misspelling shows an unreasonable, chaotic attempt bearing little relationship to any other word in the English language. It might seem that this book is therefore concerned only with the child with severe spelling difficulties but this is not so. There are many, many children within the normal school setting who are experiencing overwhelming difficulties with spelling. The following are some of the many examples I found from my own research, which investigated among other things the spelling ability of nine to ten year olds. All of these children could speak English fluently, were able to read satisfactorily according to their school's requirements, and were only slightly below average in the ordinary school subjects.

Examples of misspelling of the word 'through'
tought, fruw, thinw, throuth, throwe, teuwteuw, threou, throght, thruw, thowing, thogth, thoghe, thruwe, thoght, thgthy, thgagt, thoth, frau, froow, frou, threr, frur, thougw, thouw, thuoth, thower, thorw, thauw

4

One of the most interesting aspects I have found from my research is the tremendous depth of spelling disability found below the conventional zero mark which is accorded to those who are unable to spell any of the test words correctly. The children's spelling knowledge, as illustrated by their chaotic misspellings, is so sparse as to make the conventional spelling lesson mumbo-jumbo for them. They lack understanding of the basic knowledge which divides reasonable attempts at a word from those which bear very little relationship to any English word, such as 'thgthy' quoted above.

To the layman it may seem impossible that such weird misspellings could come from normal children, but many teachers can confirm that they are frequently faced with such problems in the course of their daily classroom teaching.

There have been many attempts by researchers to find common causes for seemingly normal, or even bright children, failing miserably in spelling. Left-handedness, cross-lateral dominance, poor vision or hearing, brain damage, low verbal ability and the like have been considered as causes of spelling disability but so far there is no clear-cut evidence to suggest why these children fail.

From the examples of misspellings given above, one common factor however seems obvious – these children display muddled thinking about the spelling task and what is expected of them. Why should they be muddled? Why has the school not helped them? These nine to ten year olds have been exposed to schooling for at least four years, and yet they do not seem to understand the basis of the task. Should we perhaps be looking at the schools and their teaching of spelling, rather than wondering what is wrong with the child? If the teaching of spelling is found to be efficient then it is reasonable to consider the problems as lying with the particular child, but first the school itself must be examined.

To date there do not seem to be many studies which investigate systematically the way spelling is taught in schools. Spelling seems to be an *ad hoc* activity in most schools. How many schools allocate definite time for the teaching of spelling? By this I mean *teaching*, and not the ritual testing of spelling which takes place in many schools each Friday morning. How many schools allocate resources for spelling? How many schools give one teacher responsibility for spelling in order to co-ordinate the teaching throughout the school? Some schools have a spelling curriculum (not just a list of words for each year), but such schools are in the minority.

On the other hand, how much help do schools receive? How many teachers receive direct help in the teaching of spelling by in-service courses, co-operation of advisers, or spelling courses whilst at college? How many college lecturers would feel capable of offering spelling courses? And as far as learning to spell is concerned, it seems very much a matter of sink or swim, with most learners succeeding somehow, after much floundering around.

Before considering *how* a child learns to spell, we must first clear away some of the myths surrounding spelling, which of course also affect the way it is taught.

2 Myths about Spelling

The way a teacher teaches spelling reflects the way she thinks spelling is learnt, and so we will now consider the ways many people *think* spelling is learnt.

Reading and Spelling

The notion that reading aids spelling is widely accepted. Whilst this is so, the amount of assistance that reading can give is of a limited nature. Peters (1979) vividly describes the perpetuation of this misunderstanding.

'Teachers have long comforted worried parents with "Don't worry, his spelling will improve when he reads more," a statement for which there is no evidence. (There is evidence that children "catch" the spelling of about one new word in every 25 they read so obviously, with this percentage, we cannot rely on reading to improve a child's spelling)'. (*Special Education*, 5, pp. 19–21)

Reading and Word Study

Whilst reading can help to get a general outline of a word, it seldom provides the opportunity to study the internal structure of a word. In reading we perceive a word in order to understand the text. Consider the errors in both of the following:

Paris in the
the Spring

Psychology is the study of the mind,
behaviour and attetudes.

Although the errors are obvious, we read so fast that we tend to overlook mistakes in our effort to understand the meaning.

Human perception uses minimal cues in order to recognise objects, people and so on. Once an object has been recognised we fail to 'see' all its other details. Take the everyday example of seeing friends. We immediately recognise them without any 'exploration', and later we often have only a hazy idea of what they were wearing, the colour of their shoes, or whether they were carrying anything. We saw the *friends*, and as soon as recognition had been established we ceased to study them in detail. This process also applies to our perception of words.

Gray (1960) advocated teaching a child to read by presenting similar word shapes, so that
'as a child begins to encounter words that are very similar in appearance, he learns to compare their detail and to note minute differences that distinguish one word from another' (*The Reading Curriculum* p. 279). However, shortly afterwards he says
'then, too, young readers often use the initial consonant as a clue to the whole word. The initial consonant 'r', for example, combined with meaning clues from a picture may be all that a child needs to recognise the word "red" in the context "a big red car".'

This highlights one of the problems in word recognition. It is pointless to say that a child ought to develop the habit of looking at every detail of a word if, in practice, one small clue will suffice. Human perception is a rapid, efficient process.

Diack (1960) also stresses this attention to every letter in words and says
'a great many spelling mistakes are due not to ignorance of how a word should be spelt but to inability to see what is on the page, because of knowledge of the context . . . part-seeing at the early stages may take a pupil some way in reading, but can take him nowhere in spelling.' (*Reading and the Psychology of Perception* p. ix, Appendix II)

It would seem that the skills used for reading have only a limited usefulness when it comes to spelling, since a reader attends more to the meaning than the characteristics of each individual word. This is emphasised by MacKay (1976) who says
'(reading) is not recognising words so much as word meanings . . . Familiarity in this case breeds expectation.' (*Help Your Child to Read and Write and More* pp. 214–5)

Vernon (1962) makes an interesting comment upon this when she says
'a type of reading which necessitates careful attention to detail is proof-reading. . . . This is extremely difficult for most people, since they have become accustomed to overlook such details (as the exact shapes and order of letters and words in the text) . . . it can be done

only by reading very slowly, and by paying comparatively little attention to the general meaning of the text.' (*The Psychology of Perception* pp. 105–6)

If attention to letter order requires a sacrifice on the part of reading comprehension, it would seem advantageous to find another method, other than reading, in which the child can practise detailed letter perception.

Other Differences between Reading and Spelling

Besides the fact that reading is too rapid for children to note much of the internal structure of words, it must be remembered that the reading task differs quite considerably from the spelling task. Reading requires word recognition and the extraction of meaning from print; spelling, on the other hand, requires recall of words and the construction of sentences to convey meanings already present in the writer's mind. Briefly, reading can be thought of as a recognition task and spelling a task of recall.

Reading is a decoding task and spelling one of encoding. Reading allows for intelligent guesswork from clues already on the printed page, and from the child's knowledge of language, but guesswork is of little help in spelling. Wedell (1973) stresses the difference when he says

'In contrast to reading . . . the child has no scope for extrapolation – he cannot leave out words or parts of words but has to complete each detail of the code to achieve acceptable spelling. (*Learning and Perceptuo-motor Disabilities in Children* pp. 91–2)

In contrast to reading, spelling requires a high degree of exactness. It requires conformity to an adult, standard form of orthography. Another important consideration is that once a word is written it remains visible for all to judge its accuracy. If a word is mispronounced or a sentence read incorrectly, no evidence remains to remind the child of its failure.

It is common to find that a child, or adult, is perfectly able to read a word which he is unable to spell. Spelling requires greater precision throughout the whole word, not just a hazy image backed by intelligent guesswork. It is very rare indeed to find a good speller who has reading difficulty, and yet we often find spelling ability lagging behind reading ability.

Conclusion

Thus, we should not leave spelling to be caught through reading but, instead, devise activities which enable the child to concentrate upon the internal structure of words. While the word remains embedded in a sentence the context is likely to make detailed observation of the word unnecessary for the context cues aid recognition.

However, some forms of reading activities do seem to aid spelling and these will be described in later chapters. Indeed, although the difference between reading and spelling has been stressed, there is some overlap of skills. Hildreth (1959) sums up the situation as:
'The graphic symbols and the oral elements in the two cases are identical, but the mental and associative process are the reverse of each other. This means that different forms of practice for word analysis in reading and spelling are needed, even though the practice in each is mutually beneficial.' (*Teaching Reading* p. 148).

If we do not leave children to catch spelling through their reading, but instead try to teach them, how do we teach them? This leads on to probably the most widely held myth of them all – spelling rules.

Spelling Rules

Possibly the most common way of teaching spelling relies upon spelling rules. To many people, 'teaching spelling' means 'teaching spelling rules', i.e. formal statements about the way letters always behave. For example:
'When two vowels are side by side (ea, ai, ee) the first vowel says its alphabetical name and the second is silent: *treat, feet, main.*'

This apparently simple rule is still difficult for children to remember and to generalise from when confronted with an unknown word. It is, in fact, more useful for reading than spelling, although it is given as a spelling rule. If a child tried to apply this rule, would it help him to spell the words *break* or *fair*?

Many other rules relate only to the addition of suffixes or plurals:
'Double the final consonant of one-syllable words with one short vowel followed by one consonant before a suffix beginning with a vowel' (Longley 1975, *BBC Adult Literacy Handbook* p. 45), and
'words ending in "ch", "sh", "x", "z" (hissing sounds) add "es" in the plural'. So do such rules achieve their objective and help children to spell?

It is generally believed that rules do help bad spellers because they reduce the learning load in that they govern hundreds of words. The learning of a few rules and the words which illustrate them will supposedly help the bad speller conquer most of his difficulties. This is too optimistic a view and is likely to lead to further dejection and confusion on the part of the learner, for whilst hundreds of words might be governed by rules there are thousands of words which are learnt without the use of rules.

McLeod (1961) conducted a small survey to ascertain how many teachers taught spelling by rules. Of 174 Scottish teachers consulted, 67.8 per cent *did* teach spelling by rules. However, she found that of the rules provided by the teachers only six were of real value according to her criteria of:

'A. The rule must apply to a large number of words.
 B. It must have few exceptions.
 C. Statement of the rule must be simple and easily comprehended while being sufficiently exact to cover only the appropriate words.' (*Studies in Spelling* p. 125)

If only six rules can meet such criteria, it would seem that there must be a large number of spelling patterns uncatered for. For example, which rules govern the spelling of names, for these are usually the first words the children learn to spell? Next they learn to spell simple words such as *they, was, you* and *have*: which rules govern these words?

The answer is simply that rules do not cover all words and the child has to learn to spell many of the words he requires before he encounters spelling rules; hence spelling rules may be an aid to some children for some words but for most children and most words we have to look to other activities to help them learn to spell.

Parts Learning

Teachers often attempt to teach 'difficult' words by concentrating upon the most troublesome part or by dividing the word into syllables. This type of parts learning will now be considered.

'Word Families'

With this method the teacher selects words, usually from published lists, which contain common letter groups. The rationale behind this can best be illustrated by reference to the work of Livingston (1961): 'Before any profitable attempt can be made to discover how best to teach spelling, the various types of difficulties and their frequencies must first be determined. That is to say, teachers should know not only that a certain word is difficult for children but also the point in the word at which error is most frequent, and the type of error most usually introduced there.' (*Studies in Spelling* p. 160)

This makes two assumptions. Firstly, that mistakes are static, that is, exactly the same mistake is made each time, but as will be seen later (on page 18) children tend not to make the same mistake when they write the word a second time. They still may not spell the word correctly but the error is often different. The second assumption is that learners find one part of a word particularly difficult, a 'hard spot', and if the teacher concentrates upon this hard spot then the children will be able to spell the word. The following examples were collected from one class and illustrate the range of misspellings which can be found. Was there a common hard spot? With reference to Livingston (above), where is the point at which error is most frequent, and the type of error most usually introduced there?

Examples of the misspelling of the word 'search'

sugh, sherch, sercth, sturtch, serch, sart, suth, chuh, sherace, seach, seerch, surched, shearch

'Hard spots' are often termed 'families' which is rather puzzling. There is neither a heirarchy, such as a family tree, nor a unifying factor as there is in, say, a family surname. There is a common feature such as 'ie' found in words such as *field, believe, friend, chief, piece, view* and *tie*, but such words could easily have been grouped differently according to another letter group. For example, *friend* could also be placed in the family of words containing 'fr'.

The term word family contains the suggestion that words fit into one or other group, but not both. However, children should be encouraged to consider words as containing many features, and all the letters are of equal importance. After all there is no point in learning that *piece* has the 'ie' letter group if the rest of the word is not learnt; which could result in the word being spelt *pies*.

Identifying 'Hard spots'

This leads on to the question of how the teacher is to draw the pupil's attention to the hard spot. There seem to be two conflicting views. Torbe (*Teaching Spelling* 1978) suggests that attention be drawn to the most difficult part by colouring that part in felt-tip pen, but such practice was condemned by Schonell in 1942:
'No division, underlining, accents or marking with coloured chalks was used in presenting the words, since it has been found that this tends to distort the actual pattern or schema of the word and to

12

handicap the pupil in forming a natural and stable visual image.' (p. 331)

Jensen (*Journal of Educational Psychology* 1962) conducted experiments to discover which parts of words were the most difficult and he found it inadvisable to emphasise hard spots. He cites Horn (*Encyclopedia of Educational Research* 1960) who gives details of studies where difficult parts of words had been emphasised in some way, such as bold type or underlining, and it was found that this was of little or no value in increasing the probability that the word would be spelt correctly. The hard spot was admittedly learnt more quickly but the time taken to learn the whole word was not significantly improved.

Syllables

A similar parts method is to divide the word into syllables, and again this is usually done by the teacher. For long words it would seem that this might be useful especially if the word is phonically regular and the child is allowed to find the syllables for himself. However, there is no need for teachers to draw lines down to divide the word into syllables, for this distorts the total image. For example:

se|par|ate   or
par|a|llel

Also, it must be remembered that many words do not divide neatly into syllables and there is no certainty that having divided the word into syllables, each syllable will then be spelt correctly. Many short words too are stumbling blocks for the learner. How are these to be learnt if we cannot divide them into syllables? Consider the words *would*, *two*, *which* and *their*. How could the teacher divide these into meaningful parts?

Mnemonics

Another method often advocated in remedial teaching is the use of mnemonics. This method does not require the learner to generalise to unknown words but concentrates upon ways of learning 'tricky' words. This is one method recommended by the Adult Literacy Scheme and also by Wight-Boycott (1978). An example given by the latter will illustrate this method:
'Sometimes the using of the initial letter of a sentence to make a word is helpful, especially with irregular words, e.g. NECESSARY: Never Eat Cake, Eat Salmon Sandwiches And Remain Young.' (*Remedial Education* p. 103)

Obviously such a method could not work for all words as the learner would soon become overburdened with the task of remembering numerous sentences.

Another important point to consider which applies to the use of rules as well as mnemonics is that the learner has to learn an intermediate task *before* being able to concentrate upon the word itself. Both these methods would seem a step backwards from the final activity where letters flow from the pen automatically. The learner has to make a conscious effort to recall something else before he can start writing the word. Any method which impedes the seemingly automatic flow of writing needs to be treated with caution. It might be useful as an aid to overcoming a 'hitch' but not as a general method to teach all spelling.

Phonic Spelling

How often are learners told to analyse the word into its component sounds and then simply write these down? Obviously a child who is able to do this will give some sort of spelling, and in some cases he may even be right, but it is a myth to suggest that spelling is simply writing down the sounds of a word.

Let us return to the reading task to see how this misunderstanding might have arisen. Blending is a skill used in reading whereby the learner analyses each letter sound and then runs them together so as to blend them into a word. For example, *c-a-t* blends together to form *cat*, and *w-e-n-t* blends together to form *went*. But what do *h-a-v-e* or *y-o-u-r* blend together to form? Obviously some words lend themselves to blending and others do not. Teachers who teach reading by a phonic method only conveniently overlook this, just as teachers who say they teach spelling by a phonic method must also turn a blind eye to the fact that many words are not phonic renderings. One cannot simply reverse the blending process in order to spell all words, although it is possible in some cases and this is a useful starting point, especially for young learners.

Phonic analysis is required in reading, and obviously some phonic training is necessary in spelling, particularly with regard to the consonants. However, the position of the letter within the word gives more indication of the sound it represents (if the letter represents any sound at all, silent letters being not uncommon in English). This positioning is particularly true with vowels: for in the word *position* the 'i' before the 't' has a different sound to the 'i' after the 't'. Even with consonants there is no easy sound/letter correspondence: 'h' in the words *health* or *through*, or 'c' in *circus* or 'g' in *gigantic*.

14

Accordingly, as Peters (1979) says with regard to spelling
'We must forget about the sound and concentrate on letter strings'
(p. 20). Also MacKay (1978) says
'It is, therefore, important that in teaching about spelling we do not
attempt to relate symbols only to sounds, as in traditional phonic
teaching. There is much more than this to teach about spelling.'
(*Breakthrough to Literacy* p. 130). As Thompson (*Learning to Read. A
Guide for Teachers and Parents* 1970) neatly sums it up
'Phonic spelling . . . is often wrong spelling.'
Should there still be those who believe that we write as we speak,
the following poem may give food for thought:

Hints on Pronunciation for Foreigners

I take it you already know
Of tough and bough and cough and dough?
Others may stumble but not you,
On hiccough, thorough, laugh and through.
Well done! And now you wish, perhaps,
To learn of less familiar traps?

Beware of heard, a dreadful word
That looks like beard and sounds like bird,
And dead: it's said like bed, not bead —
For goodness' sake don't call it 'deed'!
Watch out for meat and great and threat
(They rhyme with suite and straight and debt).
A moth if not a moth in mother
Nor both in bother, broth in brother,
And here is not a match for there
Nor dear and fear for bear and pear
And then there's dose and rose and lose —
Just look them up — and goose and choose,
And cork and work and card and ward,
And font and front and word and sword,
And do and go and thwart and cart —
Come, come, I've hardly made a start!
A dreadful language? Man alive.
I'd mastered it when I was five.
T.S.W.
from a letter in *The Sunday Times*, January 3rd, 1965

Thus *some* phonic teaching is necessary but the child has to learn, even in the early stages, not to rely totally on auditory analysis. In spelling he has to learn to trust his eye more than his ear. Visual perception is one of the most important factors to be considered when learning to spell. Auditory analysis is useful in that it can narrow down the possible choices of letters but it is only by studying the word visually that the learner can be certain of the correct spelling.

Classification of Poor Spellers

This leads on to another myth which bedevils the teaching of spelling – the belief that poor spellers use strategies which indicate their underlying weakness. It is believed these weaknesses have to be diagnosed and then special teaching has to be given to eradicate these deficiencies.

Schonell (1942) for example, gives six classifications which he lists in a chapter on 'Causes of Disability in Spelling'. His six causes are:

1. weak visual ability
2. weak auditory ability
3. both
4. feeling of inferiority
5. speech defects and faulty pronunciation
6. carelessness.

There is a certain amount taken for granted in this sort of classification, and there is still the belief that you can diagnose according to the types of errors that a child makes. For example, if a child spells the word *brought* as *bought*, does this indicate weak auditory ability, faulty pronunciation, or mere carelessness? Since Schonell's classifications, various other classifications of errors have been suggested, but all need to be treated with caution.

It is difficult to be certain whether an error falls into one category or another. It is also interesting to note that whilst the below might appear to be examples of the work of five different poor spellers they are, in fact, ten spelling errors from the same child's test paper.

Although it makes for 'neater' teaching if we can group children according to a disability, are we really certain that such grouping actually aids the teaching of spelling? We could, after all, group according to height or weight and this would divide the learners into classified groups but is there a relationship between height and weight, and spelling ability? If the results of a spelling test indicated

16

that a child wrote *cof* for *cough*, does this mean he has weak visual ability, or does it simply mean that he did not know how to spell the word and this was the nearest approximation he could give?

What percentage of errors of one classification would be necessary in order to diagnose the child's cause of spelling disability? Do some words lend themselves more to auditory errors and others to visual errors? Are such classifications really causes of spelling disability or are they merely manifestations of a general spelling difficulty?

Examples of classification of poor spellers
1. *Weak visual ability*

dorter

(daughter)

wurey

(worry)

2. *Weak auditory ability*

Sper

(spare)

Bran

(brain)

3. *Possibly both 1 and 2*

rimon

(remain)

hed ack

(headache)

4. *Faulty pronunciation*

coth

(cough)

damiJs

(damage)

5. *Carelessness*

ented

(entered)

mistak

(mistake)

17

My own studies have indicated that poor spellers vary their mis-spellings considerably, as if groping for the one which looked right. The following illustrate the types of errors made in three tests:

Word: HEALTH

Pupil	Test 1	Test 2	Test 3
1	helfe	helf	helth
2	help	helef	helth
3	hlth	halth	health
4	heath	heth	heathl
5	hepth	hleath	heath
6	haf	hefth	heath
7	hefer	helfer	healf
8	helath	hethel	health

Although more work needs to be done on this fluidity of errors it does seem to indicate that any diagnosis made upon the results of just one spelling test may be misleading, as errors seem to fluctuate. It was also found that correct spellings emerged and disappeared in subsequent tests in an inexplicable way. This means that any classifications might also vary. A child classified as a 'weak visualiser' might, on a second test be classified as having 'weak auditory ability'. Before we start on any programme which is designed to assist a particular type of speller we have to be certain that, indeed, children *can* be classified in this way.

A Method of Spelling

This is possibly the most serious myth of all but it affects other educational subjects as well as spelling. Many teachers attempt to find the 'right' way to teach, but there is no one right way. Instead, there are many which the skilled teacher is able to draw upon in the light of the school organisation, the particular children in her class, and her own teaching philosophies. For teaching is an art which applies just as much to spelling as to any other subject on the curriculum. As one teacher remarked
'If only there was one way to teach . . . wouldn't it be easy . . . (and as an afterthought added) . . . and wouldn't it be boring!'

There used to be a controversy over 'phonic' or 'look-and-say' methods of teaching reading. As early as 1938 Dewey commented upon this type of polarisation as follows:
'Mankind likes to think in terms of extreme opposites. It is given to formulating its beliefs in terms of EITHER-ORS, between which it recognises no intermediate possibilities.' (*Experience and Education* p. 1)

It is as though teachers were so unsure of themselves they had to align themselves to one camp or another. Admittedly teaching is an uncertain activity; one is buffeted from all sides by political and social pressures, what works for one teacher does not work for another, and the idiosyncratic personalities of the pupils add to the complexity of the situation. With such variety from all sides there is understandably the temptation to feel secure with one 'right' method.

However, teachers now realise that a multi-approach is better. If the teacher possesses knowledge of the subject, she is then able to vary her approach according to the external conditions. The following is therefore not a description of *one* method but instead a consideration of the spelling process. If the teacher finds this analysis acceptable, then she will be able to understand the usefulness or otherwise of spelling activities. She will be able to judge the value of an activity in the light of her pupils' requirements and their particular stage in the whole process of learning to spell. The activities have a multi-approach to spelling: sometimes stressing the visual aspect, sometimes encouraging auditory analysis, and sometimes developing motor skills and the rather neglected search skills.

Before we consider the spelling process it should be noted that we are here concerned only with functional spelling, that is, learning to spell words which the learner requires in his writing. Some studies have concentrated upon generalising spelling knowledge so that the learner is able to spell pseudowords, but such learning is only of hypothetical interest. The teacher and learner in the classroom do not require this sort of knowledge. They will be quite content if they can reach the more modest goal of finding ways of remembering how to spell words which *are* within the child's vocabulary.

3 How do we Learn to Spell?

The Pre-Spelling Stage

As an adult it is difficult to imagine what the task feels like for the complete beginner. No matter how poor our own spelling is we have, nevertheless, amassed an amazing amount of information which helps us to spell. The young child possesses very little of this knowledge and therefore in order to try and imagine their starting position the reader should carry out the following tasks.

Task 1

Imagine you are trying to spell this word:

Take one quick glance at it. Now try to write it down from memory.

Result Did you start writing the word from left to right or from right to left? In this particular 'language' we have to write from right to left, so that is one point to be learnt.

Was one quick glance sufficient to remember it all? From this one encounter with the word do you think you could remember it tomorrow, next week and next year?

This is somewhat similar to the task facing the young child. He is unfamiliar with the components of the word and does not realise that words have to be written and read in one direction only. Obviously if we can learn these two points we are in a position to *start* learning to spell. We will now concentrate on these two aspects.

Considering first the components ('letters') of the word, what is the best way of learning these new shapes? Should we look intently at them? Should we watch another person write them, or should we take one component at a time and try to copy it? There is no one way of answering these questions but perhaps you might like to discover your own answers by undertaking the next task.

Task 2

Consider the first component and learn it in your own preferred way or ways.

Result The component you should have been practising was 6 because we are working from right to left. How did you learn the 'letter'? Did you try more than one method? How many attempts did you make?

With regard to the first 'letter', did you in fact revert to the English convention of working from left-to-right? It is easy to forget the directional requirement, particularly when your mind is concentrating upon another new component of the task, but in the early stages this is quite acceptable and does not suggest some sort of brain malfunction although this is still occasionally suggested. Direction is a convention which has to be learnt; that is all there is to it.

Now let us consider how you learnt the 'letter'. Personally, I find copying the most effective way. At first the copying is slow, painfully slow, as I falter at each turn of the pen, but gradually it becomes more flowing until I am able to perform the task without looking at the master copy. Some of the more imaginative might have made the shape in plasticine or clay. Some might have drawn it in the air or traced it on the table. Although the latter examples might have worked for you, I prefer to see the efforts of my labour and therefore might use these last activities as a check after learning the symbol by writing it, but first I would copy it.

Occasionally copying is decried by teachers and I would agree that copying in the later stages should be discouraged, but in the very early stages when the task is one of learning symbols it seems to be one of the most effective ways of learning.

How many times did you need to practise it? It does not matter if it was only once or many, many times. The main thing is: did you learn it? This means not just for now, but would you be able to write it from memory tomorrow, or next week? Obviously, the more often you write it, particularly if followed by short revision periods spread over many weeks, then the more likely you are to commit it to memory. However, it is very much a personal matter and each learner would have to practise the 'letter' for as many times as he required, not a specified number of times given by the teacher. The learner must be responsible for his own learning, even in the early stages.

Task 3

Now look back at the word given in Task 1. Give yourself about the same amount of time for studying the word, that is a quick glance, and try once more to write the word.

Result Was it slightly easier this time? Did you again make the mistake of direction or are you on the way to learning this rule?

How much time did you spend studying the first symbol ᶜᶜ ?

It is more than likely that you spent very little time on the first symbol since you were already familiar with the shape and were therefore able to concentrate upon the more unfamiliar symbols. Is this not very similar to the way a young learner progresses? Having once learnt the shape of a symbol he does not waste time on it, but simply checks that it is indeed the same as the symbol he has been learning and not an almost identical one, then progresses to the next symbol. If, by any chance, the young learner should know all the symbols then he can naturally enough spend his time concentrating upon order, not the shape of each symbol.

Summary of Pre-spelling Stage

Thus we can summarise this early stage as one where the learner becomes familiar with the letter shapes. The more practice he gets in making the shapes, perhaps using different media such as clay, chalk etc., the more likely it is that the symbols will be well and truly learnt. Just because the teacher is familiar with the letter shapes she should not underestimate the amount of time and practice required by the learner. Plenty of time spent at this stage will mean that the later stages will be learnt more smoothly and quickly, for no-one can learn to spell unless he is truly familiar with the shapes of the symbols. All this may seem obvious, but some children of nine and ten years still exhibit confusion over letter shapes, which seems an unnecessary added burden when they are also trying to grapple with order.

Besides learning the shape of the symbol it is also important to give it a name, for labelling helps to identify and distinguish it from all other symbols. However, in the early stages it should be remembered that this is *only* a label; it might also indicate a possible 'sound' for this letter, but there is a certain ambiguity between letter shapes and letter sounds which is not always appreciated by the teacher of spelling. So in the early stages concentrate upon the learning of the letter shapes.

Order Stage

The next stage, which overlaps the first, is that of order. How can the learner remember which symbol goes next?

The earlier stage concentrated upon letter shape and whilst the letter label should not necessarily be though of as representing the letter sound, nevertheless, the child at some point will realise that there is some connection. The ideas of letter shapes and sounds should not be thought of as mutually exclusive. Whilst the letter does not necessarily represent a sound, nevertheless it often does do so. If the teacher is not dictatorial in her attitude towards letters and sounds, then the children will soon learn to accept both ideas.

This means that one way of learning the order of letters in a word is to go by the sound the symbols represent. This of course cannot be applied to all words but it should be exploited whenever the word has a close sound/symbol correspondence.

The learner should be encouraged to consider new words firstly from the point of view of whether or not they can be written as they sound. Many words can be written entirely on a phonic basis and the child should be encouraged to gain confidence in his ability to analyse a word into its sounds and then merely slot in the correct symbols. Almost all words have at least some part of them which have a close sound/symbol correspondence, and therefore the skill of auditory analysis is important in learning to spell.

However, the child soon has to learn that it is not always as simple as that. It does not mean to say that a phonic spelling is definitely wrong but that it can be, and often is, wrong. The child has to learn that auditory analysis is useful but cannot be totally relied upon, in other words it has to be used with caution, and seldom supersedes the ability to *look* carefully at the internal structure of words. When a learner is confronted with a new word he wishes to commit to memory he should have a debate with himself, asking such questions as 'Can it be spelt as it sounds?' If not, 'Can some of it be spelt as it sounds?' The learner has to make the decision according to his own knowledge of symbols and the way he speaks.

The learner's knowledge of symbols is thus more complex than just knowing the label for each letter and this takes us on to the next task.

23

Task 4

Looking back at our original word given in Task 1, it would seem that we have six symbols to learn. The second symbol is called 'ka' and is always followed by the third symbol 'w', although it should be noted that this third symbol has a different sound when standing alone. This might sound rather complicated so it is suggested that you learn both symbols together, which is made more easy by the fact that with a bit of imagination the symbols combine to look like a boot kicking a ball. Now try learning the combined symbol by whatever method suits you.

Now try to identify this combined symbol in the following words:

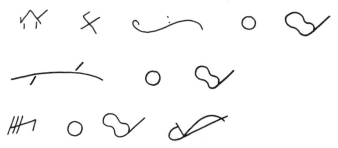

Result Was this an easy task? Was it made easier because you were now familiar with the combined symbols? Looking back at the original word do you now think that you would see both symbols separately or would you recognise them as a pair, i.e. one chunk of information?

Most learners would now 'see' the original word as being composed of five symbols, not six as was formerly supposed. Seeing in chunks like this makes it easier to recall the components of a word, for once a chunk is learnt then this is handled as one symbol and there is then less to remember. This aids recall of correct ordering.

We will now leave our fictitious word composed of pseudo-symbols and look towards the way we spell in English. However, we are still concerned with learning in chunks.

The simplest for the child to learn are letter pairs, such as 'sh', 'ch', 'th', 'wh', 'er' and 'st'. Whilst all of these happen to represent phonic units the patterns should also be considered visually. If the 'ou' pair is considered it is best merely to study them as letters which often come together. Telling the child that they 'say' 'ou' can be very confusing for the child who then sees the letter pair in words like 'could' and 'you'. Getting the child to see letters as forming chunks may aid auditory analysis but it should be more than that; it should lead to a closer visual examination of new words

24

in the hope of finding chunks already familiar to the learner. Remember that learning the pseudo-symbol pair (the ball being kicked) not as two symbols but only as one, facilitated recall and also recognition amongst other fictitious words.

There is no precise order for learning these chunks, as it all depends upon the child's background. For example, if his name is Richard he might be more interested in 'ch' or 'ar' letter pairs, than Peter who would probably be more interested in the 'er' pair, and if they both lived in Ealing they might both well start with an interest in 'ea', or the 'ing' letter group.

The child should not be required to learn the words which contain these letter groups – merely to note that the 'chunks' are there. This type of search means that, besides becoming familiar with a letter group, the learner is practising the essential skill of examining the internal structure of words. When a child is familiar with a letter group, or even a letter, then this stands out from the rest and makes it easier for him to recall it. James (1890) wrote that cognitive life begins when one is able to exclaim, 'Hello! Thingummybob again.' (*The Principles of Psychology 1890*). Having first become familiar with something we are then able to recognise it instantly. In spelling, once we have enough knowledge of letters and letter groups to recognise them instantly in other words, then we are on the way to learning to spell.

This grouping into familiar combined symbols is largely idiosyncratic to each language. Each language has its own way of using symbols. For example, which is the English word in the following list?

1. llanwry
2. xerozski
3. thousting

Actually there is no English word present in the list for they are all pseudo-words, but number three is more like an English word than the others. The reason is that the letter grouping is similar to that found in many English words. If you were able to identify number three as the most likely one to be English then you are familiar with the English coding system. A 'coding system' refers to the way we group information into a schema; in this case letters into groups which are then stored as chunks. The term 'coding system' will be used from now on to describe the way we group letters into 'chunks' according to our own language.

Obviously if the learner has a great deal of knowledge of the particular coding system in use then a quick glance at a word means that he will be able to identify large chunks and remember these easily. However, another learner, who does not possess this knowledge of the coding system, will have to remember the order of each separate symbol. Not only will the latter find the task more difficult, but the probability of error will be greater.

In 1942 Gilbert and Gilbert (*University of California Publications in Education*), made an extensive study of eye-movements recorded by use of a camera while the learner scanned a word presented on a flashcard. The person was told that he was to learn the word so that he could write it correctly after the study period. It seems reasonable to suppose that the eye-movements made under these conditions closely resemble those made when learning to spell a new word.

It was particularly interesting that good and poor spellers showed marked differences in the way they tackled the problem. Character-istic features of the poor speller included a greater number of oscilla-tions back and forth across the word, frequent repetitions of part study of the word and an unusually high number of fixations (pauses). It seems that the poor speller concentrates upon detailed analysis of letters in a rather haphazard fashion. The good speller, on the other hand, seemed to recognise familiar sequences and so concentrated in a more systematic way upon difficult spots.

Apparently, then, the poor speller tackles a new word letter by letter, while the good speller recognises 'chunks' and is able to spend time studying any unusual letters or letter groups. The whole process is one of verification based upon the learner's knowledge of the English coding system.

It will be noticed that the emphasis is firmly on visual perception. As mentioned earlier, although auditory analysis is useful it is only by looking carefully at a word that we can be certain of its correct spelling.

The learner has to develop the habit of looking carefully at each section of a word and weighing it up in the light of what he expected to find there. When looking at a new word the learner should be asking himself questions such as 'How much of it can be written as it sounds?' 'Are there any silent letters?', 'Are there any new letter groups which I have not encountered before?', 'Ah! There's thing-ummybob again – I know that one!' And if it is a new word for his vocabulary he should be asking 'What does it mean?', 'How do you pronounce it?'

Asking such questions directs attention to the components of a word and makes the studying period purposeful. With a competent speller this intense visual inspection of a word is all that is required for the word to be committed to memory. However, most learners also require practice in writing the word, for this is the acid test of learning. The learner can think he knows the spelling but it is only when he has to try and reproduce it that he is aware of hazy sections, usually in the middle of the word.

Reproducing a word by writing it is an important stage in learning to spell, although it is often given scant attention in schools. We spell in order to write, so writing should be the goal. Also, although the word has been committed to memory in chunks it now has to be reproduced letter by letter, and the order of letters in a word signifies an order in time. Writing the word also reinforces the need to examine words closely, for the position of every letter is important.

Summary of the Order Stage

The pre-spelling stage consisted in becoming *familiar* with the symbols, both their names and their shapes. When the learner was familiar with symbols he could *recognise* them instantly. These two aspects should be thought of as running concurrently – the first symbols which are now truly learnt will be recognised immediately while other symbols are still being mastered.

The order stage is knowledge of the coding system, which means learning the correct order of letter groups or 'chunks'. These letter groups are peculiar to each language. It is a long and complex stage, ranging from simple letter pairs to almost complete words such as 'ough' in 'cough' or 'ought'. As at the symbol stage, so each letter group will require a lengthy period of *familiarisation* followed by a rapid *recognition* stage.

Word Stage

Just as most learners find it necessary to practice reproducing a new symbol many times before they feel mastery over it, so the same applies to writing whole words. The more often the person writes it from *memory*, the more confident he will become about the correct order of every letter in the *whole* word.

During the word stage the child will learn to look at whole words in an effort to recall each and every part of it. He will not study a word as an example of a spelling rule, or examine just that part of the word which indicates a hard spot. Instead he will study all of it in a methodical way, using his knowledge of the coding system so that his learning is efficient.

27

Finally, the word should be used in written context for it to be truly learnt. As a parallel, imagine you have just added a new word to your vocabulary. You have learnt its meaning and how to pronounce it but never have occasion to use it. Most likely you will forget the word and the effort spent on learning it has been largely wasted. The same applies to learning to spell, and just as saying the word once or twice will not usually fix a new word in our spoken vocabulary, so writing the word in a few exercises will seldom fix the correct spelling. We truly learn only those words which we are likely to require, and by using them we strengthen our learning – the rest remains rather 'wobbly'.

This applies to children the same as to adults; the more you write, the more likely you are to be a competent speller, and being a competent speller your knowledge of the coding system will be sharpened so that new words are learnt all the more easily. Once a person has sufficient skill to write freely they usually enjoy writing, which gives them more practice in the skill and so it goes on. In my experience I have always found good spellers love writing and spelling. Is it just coincidence that those who like writing also are competent spellers ? Surely it is just the same as with other skills – we enjoy what we are good at and shy away from our incompetence in other things – thus making failure in these even more likely.

Learning to spell therefore must involve writing and plenty of it.

Summary of the Word Stage

The word stage permeates all the previous stages but becomes more prominent towards the end of the coding stage. However, it should be stressed that there is no point in learning first all the symbols in isolation, and then all the letter groups in isolation, without referring these to actual words. Symbols and letter groups become meaningful only in relation to actual words and the learner should be encouraged to discover words containing his new symbol or letter group. In this way his learning will become more positive, purposeful and interesting.

Finally, a word of warning should be given to any teacher who thinks that learning can be neatly compartmentalised, for unfortunately this is seldom so. Learning is a rather messy business. The child's interests, aptitudes and backgrounds influence what he will learn and when. The skilled teacher will use these factors to the child's advantage and this can be applied to spelling just as any other subject. Spelling should be thought of as a discovering activity stemming from the child's interests, rather than a set of rigid exercises.

28

4 Jacqueline Learns to Spell

Very little seems to be known about the way young children learn to write. Children write words from memory long before they are formally taught spelling at school. They acquire most of their early words without any use of rules or knowledge of phonics, so how do they do it? The following gives an examaple of how one child, Jacqueline, acquired some of the basic requirements of spelling before the age of five years. She was not taught in the generally accepted sense, but instead was stimulated through motor activities.

Jacqueline is in no way unusual. However, as this is the study of only one child the reader should beware of generalising too widely from these examples. The examples were collected from the child's own spontaneous writing over a period of two years.

The first examples (**a**) were collected in the month before her third birthday. Among the scribble we can see a 'J' sprinkled liberally around the page, in fact, I believe there are seventeen 'J's. Previously she had been allowed to write over the 'J' of her name when sending birthday cards etc. to members of her family. She had, therefore, even at this early age participated in a functional writing activity. About this time she made the connection that a 'J' signified her name and hence the delight in repeating her 'name' all over the page.

Almost a year later, at the age of three years ten months she completed the page of writing (**b**). By now she had taught herself many other letters besides her 'J' and from this crowded page we sense a feeling of her pride in her prowess. Nobody had asked her to do this task; she did it because she enjoyed doing it. By looking carefully, and with a little imagination, it is possible to see many words. They do flow in different directions, such as *cup* and *elephant* but she, herself, probably had little idea that she was writing words. She was, in fact, copying the letters and therefore the words from the Ladybird ABC book.

a

By now she was firmly established as a left-hander, at least in writing, but it is unlikely that her change of direction in words like *cup* and *elephant* was anything more serious than a desire to fit the letters in, or the fact that she could see her progress if she wrote from right to left. These sorts of reversals are very common in young children whether they are left or right handed, and should certainly not be considered symptomatic of some serious deficiency. It is merely a matter of learning the requirements of the task, one of which is the directional left to right flow of writing.

Often Jacqueline could be found filling pages with letters. She did not ask what the letters said, but obviously knew they had some connection with the world around her, for she would study cereal packets, street names and so on for letters she could recognise. Consequently they had to be identified in some way and so gradually she learnt the names for many letters.

Often warnings are given to parents that they must not call letters by their alphabetical names, such as 'a-ch' for 'H' but rather make the sound 'h', the warning sometimes being given the other way

round. Personally I usually give the child both labels on different occasions, for contrary to the above opinions, the child is able to accept many names for the same object without losing sight of the fact that the object remains the same, so that Mummy, who is a lady or woman, is also Mrs . . ., Darling, Jill, etc. With regard to the labels for letters a child is seldom confused by two similar labels, but can easily be confused by the adult who tells him, 'No, it's not an 'a-ch' but a 'h'. This is petty and dishonest for both labels are correct. If the child wants to know the different names of a letter, by all means tell him for there is no evidence yet to suggest that a learner becomes confused by learning both labels or that one label is superior to another.

At this point it might also be worth considering the shapes of letters, and especially the fuss made about capital letters. Many first schools have a policy which regulates the type of print to be used throughout the school. This is not just a suggested handwriting style but rather dictates exactly the form of, say, 'l' to be used by staff and pupils alike. At first glance, this might seem quite reasonable, but it is sometimes carried to extremes and the children are reprimanded if they use the wrong form, thus confusing the child.

If a common print is to be used in order to familiarise the child with just one form so that he does not become confused, it is a good starting point, but it is *only* a starting point. As soon as the child shows he is able to be introduced to other forms, or has already encountered different forms in his everyday life, then the opportunity should be seized on by the teacher to encourage that child to find different forms of letters.

To stick rigidly to one style of print is to deny the fact that the child will meet other forms outside of school. Let the school utilise the child's exploring instinct and gradually build up the child's knowledge of various forms of letters.

In order to see whether there was a common 'a' used in our everyday life, I made a small survey throughout one day noting every 'a' I encountered. The most common 'a' was not the 'ɑ' which is usually taught in schools but the 'a' which was found on railway signs and many sweet and biscuit wrappers. Next in popularity was the capital 'A' which was used in street names and many packets of food.

This leads onto the antagonism sometimes found in schools about capital letters. 'Don't teach them capital letters', I have heard said. Why not? What evidence is there that the child will not need capital letters? In fact, if you look around you you will find a surprising number of examples where capital letters only are used. Also, it must be remembered that in the beginning the child is usually intently interested in his own name, so are you to write it all in lower case, which is incorrect, or should you include the initial capital letter, in which case the child is going to learn a capital letter first as the initial letter makes more impression than any of the other symbols? Since the child will need capital letters at some point let him use them as and when they occur naturally.

It would seem that we should encourage the young child to write whenever possible, so that it becomes an enjoyable activity, and not one fraught with restrictions. It will be seen from Jacqueline's early writing that it was a pleasant activity otherwise she would never have written spontaneously nor filled every page to overflowing.

On her fourth birthday she was given two presents which greatly stimulated her to write. One gift was a set of felt-tipped pens and the other gift a Mr Men writing set. The combination of these two presents can be seen in example (c). She was so stimulated by these gifts that she continued to write and write until all the paper was used and everyone in the family had received many letters. Nearly all the letters said the same thing; however the important thing was not the message but the fact that she was using her writing for a task she considered worth doing. And so she had reached the stage where she realised that letters combined into words and these words could be read by other people.

In the beginning she had to ask for the spelling of every word. These were merely written on a slip of paper which she copied from. Within a very short time she was able to write much of the sentence herself, but it should be remembered that nearly all the messages were the same and with so much repetition it was fairly easy to remember the spellings. However sometimes her writing requirements were very ambitious. Example (**d**) arose from watching her brother complete some biology homework. Her caption reads, 'a person's bones and veins'.

Every opportunity for writing was explored by the child. The little slip of paper (**e**) was a shopping list which shows some bananas and a letter 'B' above it. She did this entirely on her own which illustrates that at the age of four she was able to analyse some sounds and give their correct letter. Like all the activities, this was not the result of teaching but purely spontaneous endeavours on the part of the child.

That Christmas she copied her complete name on all cards and even wrote all the gift tags for her own family. The writing was very untidy but it kept her happy and made her feel important, especially when she saw people reading her work.

She used pencil or pen and frequently chalked on her blackboard and on the garden path. She was also allowed to explore an old portable typewriter and (**f**) is the result of one session when she was four years two months. It might at first seem as though she had not learnt very much from this typing, but she was becoming familiar

e

f

```
          abnl  ,mgmmbtht g yhyhyhy7 7 njjj g   uu y hnn voxx zs
 k ht j  ikt nj g mm j ymtitetjtyhkk6o gh 757  mmytggtget tujnn hfu fjfjrj mgn nnt
kfjdom jgitmgtypy  y t g ykf  y ,t,h h, yi  h     mgf v gb gi ghi  r jt
jtjt j u i  t t tgft rvfjrirhf juy nhfrhrhf jrnrrrhh htnr jgjfmrjtjjt f jjrk tmgnfhbrh rjf fjgjt
rrf i tkgjtjt kt r f th n5 mtrjtr67 5nyu6 56yukd i6  4rer ru6u ut utjg r jrjjjttjttrrr rr
jfrrrnfkry vhrhrjfjrmtkrj,i dkf mjjgkfmyjrrh u5 y32345678 9 p0 we r tyu iilhhg gfdrhdbfdbh hh
 ktl   mej jd u rt tgrfft hrtrtitgjrkf v jmt  tio5 j htj rri t t jr i ggrt i kmgmmmtmbmmjijj

 mg gt , g          fnr gd j vm kf f jr g g g fjm,

 fttkgf g g yy  gt n mvt        GJM U J d f fRgRJRr F b t, r f h f vb tvnt HHR RNRrJT NR JU Y&
g GJJJJ J o(o Y JI  HJYYY G T __  U  II FGTR Y  TT  KT FVRITITTJTTU I IT
 GGH U HMTKT FTKg MYJHT T  GDJRURI HRY T Y P TRdH JHRN RHH FR UH Y WYYY YYY
 DFV UURIRITUF T FUTUT OUTUUTJRU R  CU&RU FHFU
```

with all the letters of the alphabet in lower case and capitals. She also experimented with numbers, and possibly became aware of lines and the fact that the typewriter worked in a left to right direction.

Gradually, throughout her fourth year, she asked for more and more words and very seldom indulged in filling pages with random letters.

When she was four and a half years old she was given a small stapler and, about the same time, she bought a picture stencil set from a jumble sale. The combination of these two presents resulted in the unexpected 'writing book' stage and example (**g**) is a spread from the first book. She wrote many books again at her own instigation. At this stage it was seldom necessary to give her any spellings – the common words she knew and wrote very quickly – the other words she would ask whether they had 'tricks' in them and if they did not she would analyse the word into its sounds and write the appropriate letters. Only 'trick' words were still given on slips of paper.

g

She wanted To geT The Spider
band The masTer
wash very &
qLeased.

Jacqueline was now attending part-time schooling and obviously the whole spelling process was gelling. Writing was understood by her to have a function and to be on the whole a reasonable activity. It was also an intensely enjoyable activity. Perhaps, to some, Jacqueline's spelling knowledge is very sparse, but it should be borne in mind that the above examples were all from a pre-school child, and there had been no effort to teach her to spell. She was an ordinary child who spent a lot of time doing ordinary child-like things but between all her various activities she had been teaching herself to write.

Conclusion

This pre-spelling stage was a very slow, long process but a vital one which had to be worked through at the child's own pace. Once she knew how to form some letters, these could easily be recognised. She continued learning letters and their different variations, but along with this was the learning of common, or high interest words, such as 'party'. Thus symbols, order and words all merged into one continuous activity – that of writing. All the work arose from her desire to write and was occasionally sparked off by a new medium such as coloured pens, or apparatus, such as the stapler. Through her own activities she developed the all-important positive attitude towards writing, unhampered by the rules and restrictions sometimes imposed by a teacher upon a young learner.

When Jacqueline was given pre-reading activities at school, she romped through them since they largely overlapped the writing she had been doing at home. She expected these shapes to be letters, she knew letters grouped together into words and words could be read. She had learnt all these things through writing. This is not a new idea. Chomsky (*Childhood Education* 1971) reports a similar experiment where the pre-school child was encouraged to compose his own words before he could read. Chomsky suggested that this could develop a more positive approach on the part of the learner, and this was certainly found with Jacqueline.

Having considered how one pre-school child made a start on learning to spell, let us examine the work of other young children to see whether similar processes can be found. The following examples are from spontaneous writings completed by young children at home; the writings arose from the child's own wish to write and most of it was done without any help from others.

(a) *Two year old child*

Becky took considerable time and effort to complete this page of scribble (a). She was experimenting with different coloured pencils, which unfortunately do not show up on the reproduction, and it will be noticed that she not only made circular movements but also straight lines, angles, and dots and dashes. Scribble seems to be an important start in the writing process and should not be dismissed as a mindless activity; the child is learning a great deal about the tools of writing.

a Work by a two year old girl

(b) *Three year old child*

From Joanne's work we can see the beginnings of letter shapes. (b1) may appear very much like scribble but already she is trying to control the path of the pen. Her favourite letter is 'Z' which is rather unusual and she completes pages of them. (b2) shows how she corrected herself when she went wrong; the two parallel lines were the first attempt, by the side is the second which she considered still not good enough and the third attempt underneath shows her succeeding in reproducing 'Z'. (b3) shows her other favourite letter 'o' and she already seems to understand about lines of writing. The examples in (b4) shows her trying to copy her father's name with an

b *Work by a three year old girl*

b1

b2

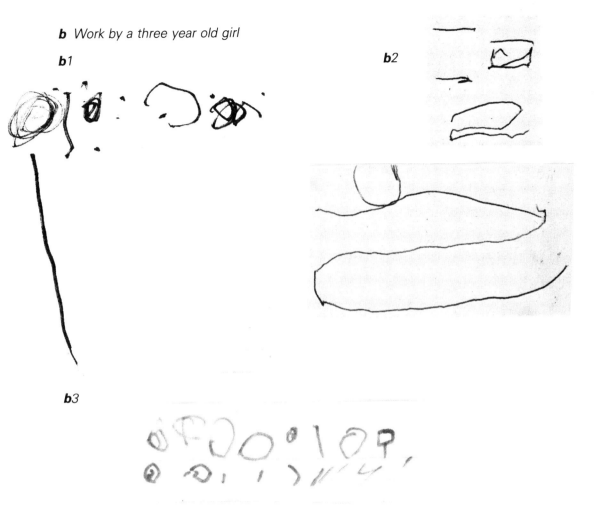

b3

'r' superimposed upon an 'a'. The 'o's are now competently made and she then decides to make some of them into people, thus showing how drawing and writing often develop side-by-side.

(c) *Four year old child*

Paul is starting to communicate on paper. The picture represents his family. He wrote his name from memory and although the letters are rather wobbly he already shows control over his pencil. The 'A' is in upper case and the 'l' in lower case; such a mixture is common even with much older children. Mixing capital letters and lower case letters is unimportant – it might be unconventional but at least the spelling is correct. Tolerance towards untidy and unusual lettering in the early stages will build up the child's confidence in himself as a writer, and it is most likely he will self-correct his handwriting when he develops a pride in himself as a 'good writer'.

(d) *Five year old child*

This is an illustration of 'play writing' which is a stage most children pass through. Angela knew how to write her own name and her cousin's name and these appear on the paper. Although she knew c *Work by a four year old boy*

d *Work by a five year old girl*

many other letters and some words she wanted to imitate the adult style and so wrote ferociously until the whole page was full. She has good control over her pen in order to complete such a long task, and we can also see that she realises writing is made up of individual letters and these are written in lines. She knew it was not real writing but just enjoyed the feel of writing; this ability to enjoy writing is often overlooked.

(e) *Six year old child*

It is said that boys frequently do not like to write. This is not true if the boy can see a purpose for his writing. Ben considered a letter to Father Christmas worth his effort and it cannot be faulted in its clarity and directness. Some of the words were copied but this was no blind copying for he knew what he was trying to convey and could read his own letter.

e Work by a six year old boy

(f) *Six year old child*

Again this boy had a purpose for writing; he had drawn a picture which he wanted to give to his grandmother, and this is the envelope he used. Although there is the minor error *two* for *to* the message comes across strong and clear. Stephen writes boldly with correct space between letters and space between words. There is still a capital 'T' in the middle of his name but he obviously knows the lower case 't' as is shown by the first word. Knowing both forms does not confuse him.

f Work by a six year old boy

PART TWO
TEACHING SPELLING

5 First Stage

Earlier it was mentioned that spelling involved familiarisation and recognition of symbol, order and words but that these were best considered as overlapping stages which merged into one activity – that of writing. The following description of teaching spelling uses all three stages concurrently, but in the early stage the symbol is given most consideration, then order becomes more important in the middle stage, and the final stage concentrates mainly upon the whole word.

In Chapter Three you were encouraged to learn a new word written in a different code in order to appreciate how difficult it is for the young child faced with an entirely new situation. Another example of adults learning a new code was studied by Bryan and Harter in 1897. In this case the code was telegraphic, that is, morse code. The investigators found that first the message was understood in terms of letters, then in words and finally in sentences. At first, the memory space was able to cope with only single letters, but with practice words were grouped in units, and so on. This is very similar to the way young children are able to learn to spell, and just like the telegraphic operators, they need plenty of practice in the activity. They cannot watch others do it but they have to do it themselves, in order to build up this knowledge of a coding system.

Especially in this early stage, the child is required to perform many activities and so discover the requirements of the task through his own efforts.

Pre-spelling

When a child first encounters spelling he is usually very young. There is no exact age when a child is ready to start learning to spell but it is, in fact, much earlier than is traditionally imagined. Since spelling in schools has usually meant just learning rules, teachers have largely been unaware of the groundwork which is necessary for spelling to make sense. Much of the following concerns the pre-school child or one just starting school. However, since the familiarisation stage continues for a long time, the following work suggestions are likely to be useful throughout the whole of the first school.

First, the child must have plenty of practice in becoming familiar with the symbols. 'Plenty of practice' does not mean watching somebody else make the letters, as when the teacher draws a letter and then says, 'What is it?' Nor does it mean handling cut-out shapes of letters although this is slightly better than the first example. Like so many other skills the only way to learn it is to do it, and in this case the child should be encouraged to make the shapes himself.

How are you to encourage the child to make letter shapes? Boys in particular often find writing irksome, and my own investigations show that boys are far more at risk in becoming atrocious spellers. If we try to confine the young child to pencil and paper, or even worse, a writing book, and make him write at a table or desk, then he is likely to lose interest. Young children seldom choose either of the above media or positions when allowed to write on their own. The aim should be to get them to enjoy writing these letter shapes so that they perform the task over and over again just for the sheer delight of it.

Most teachers are highly imaginative and are capable of devising far more effective activities for their particular children, but here at least are some starters.

Blackboards

Provide children's blackboards, about three feet long and two feet high. These blackboards can be hooked to the wall, low down, with a strip of carpet below. (This carpet enables the children to kneel in comfort and makes it easier for cleaning since the children can shake the carpet outside at the end of the day). In most classrooms you will now have difficulty getting the children to stop writing, and at least one blackboard per group is often necessary. Each group can be responsible for their own chalks and rubber. Needless to say, provide coloured chalks as well as white, for children love experimenting.

Somewhere near the blackboards should be letter shapes, so that the children are able to select a letter and practise writing it in different ways: big, little, fat, thin and in different colours. Let them explore the letters. The teacher should beware of trying to teach them how to write the letters correctly at this stage. The children should be enjoying themselves.

These blackboards can also be removed from the wall and lain flat on the tables or floor so that the children can experiment writing in different positions. It all adds to interest.

Using Everyday Materials

Other activities designed to encourage the making of letters can utilise sand trays for writing with fingers or a stick. Plasticine, clay or even pastry can be rolled into long thin strips and made into shapes. Pastry is particularly appreciated by young children since pastry letters can be baked and then eaten!

Groups can be given straws or spills and asked to find how many letters they can make with these straight items, whilst another group can be given thick wool, ribbon and string and encouraged to find as many letters as they can which are best made with 'floppy' items.

Collage Cards

In spelling we are not requiring the learner just to recognise letter shapes but to be able to write them from memory. This means that he must be aware of the basic differences between letter shapes. This can be achieved by a simple, enjoyable activity involving collage cards.

These cards should be fairly large, say A4 size, and on each card one letter is written in a bold hand. Glued to each letter shape is some

Collage cards

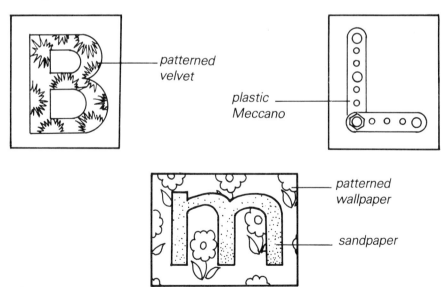

patterned velvet

plastic Meccano

patterned wallpaper

sandpaper

distinctive texture, say velvet or sandpaper. Children like to experiment by touch and so they are encouraged to run their fingers over the shape and get the general outline without any formal teaching. The children then see if they can follow the shape with their eyes closed.

This sort of activity can easily be employed in the reading scheme as well. If the teacher is introducing the children to a new letter, say the letter 'V' and they have been collecting objects starting with this letter, then the collage cards can be used to reinforce this letter shape. In the case of the 'V' it would need a strong direct material, such as corrugated paper or two pieces of Meccano. If the letter was 'S' then a thick piece of sisal or a plait of wool would be more appropriate since this would reinforce the flowing action of the letter shape. There should be nothing else upon the card, no pictures nor any attempt to make the letter shape into some connecting object, such as the 'S' into a snake. The child's eyes and fingers should be concentrating upon the shape and not be distracted by anything else.

Somewhere along the way, the children will want to know what to call these shapes, and as the need arises, so the teacher supplies the information. It doesn't really matter whether it is labelled by its alphabetical name or its sound: 'Kay' or 'k'. As the child has to learn both at some time, there is no point in making an 'either-or' issue out of it; by all means use both labels if you think the children are able to accept both. Most children are able to accept both without question, just as they are able to accept capital letters and lower case without feeling confused.

Letter Hunts

This leads on to the variety of letter shapes. The child is required to recognise letters not just in the style used by the teacher, or found in their reading books, but in the forms they are likely to encounter in their everyday lives.

Make this into a treasure hunt with the children finding as many examples of one particular letter as they can in a week. Examples showing different types of print can be pasted on a long thin strip around the classroom, again at the children's height. There can be tiny examples from the small print on the back of chocolate wrappers, to very large ones found on cereal boxes. Capital letters and lower case are all acceptable. The children are learning to recognise a letter in its various forms, sizes and colours.

This recognition stage can be run alongside the familiarisation stage

48

as each will complement the other. The children can also select their own 'letter-for-the-week', which adds to their motivation. Inform parents of the 'letter' by pinning up the letter on the classroom door or parents' noticeboard, or give the child a simple note to hand to them. Most parents are very keen to help and enjoy taking part, but they do have to be informed, and word of mouth alone is unreliable, especially as the children will forget to tell them.

Of course, much of this work will help in the teaching of reading but the emphasis here is upon the child using a motor skill to become familiar with letter shapes. He does not only have to recognise shapes (which is sufficient for the reading task) but spelling requires that he be able to make the shapes from memory. Gradually, there-fore, the teacher must wean the child away from just copying. Usually a little praise such as 'Did you write that without looking? Aren't you clever!' is all that is needed to direct his attention to the fact that eventually he will need to write letters from memory. If he is unable to write from memory, then more time is required at the familiarisation stage. Above all, remember that this early stage must not be rushed through.

Early Words

This stage creeps in before the teacher realises what is happening, which is good. Sometimes a child is found copying a whole word, or wants to write his name, and boys in particular often start by writing their favourite football team, or the name of a T.V. charac-ter. When they have copied a word it doesn't matter if they then cannot read it. Just let them continue if it keeps them happy. At the very least they are enjoying the activity of writing, and they are probably becoming aware of the fact that different symbols grouped together represent words. Both these factors will be most useful later on when the child is ready to start spelling in earnest.

When a child wants to be able to write a word, he does not choose it because it is easy or phonically regular, he wants that particular word because it has high interest value to him personally. Let him copy the word, again using any of the media mentioned above, and let him copy it many, many times. He will forget it the next day, and the next and so on, but gradually he will remember more of it at each attempt. In order to help the teacher, the child could have the word written on a small piece of card, kept in an envelope in his tidy tray. When he wants to spell 'his' word, he has a go on the black-board and checks his attempt with his card. If there are any errors, he rubs out his entire attempt and has another try. It is important that he does not slip in letters, or erase the parts which are wrong. The whole word is written again, and again, and again if necessary, until he can write the whole word quickly and surely. Each letter has to be remembered in its correct order and slipping in forgotten letters distorts this ordering.

All this is done without aid from the teacher, for children like to be able to do things on their own, and they should be encouraged right from the start to check their own spellings. These high interest words should not be made into test words – they are simply getting the child familiar with the idea that groups of letters follow one another in a set order, and make up words.

However, if the child has made good progress with letters and likes writing words, then the common word series could be started at this point. Like the high interest words mentioned above, a word is given to the child on a small personal word card. Unlike the high interest words, however, the word should be fairly simple, for these common words are going to be well and truly learnt. Examples of these common words are 'he', 'in' or 'to'. The child practises writing the word as described above.

When the child knows a word, he can then perform a recognition task such as sorting through word cards and taking out all 'his' words. This simple activity is useful in that it can be used time and time again for different words. Another recognition activity is to give the child a short piece of print, in which he has to underline the word he has been learning. Of course, he does not have to read the rest of the page, merely underline the word he knows to show that he can recognise it amongst other words.

It should be reiterated that these recognition tasks take second place to the long learning process carried out at the familiarisation stage. It is only by writing the word, and copying it in the first instance, that the child will fully learn all the letters in their correct order. With words containing only two letters this may seem unnecessary, but how often do children write 'no' for 'on' and even 'ti' for 'it'? It could be argued that the second example is not even a word but this is not apparent to the very young child, who would say that he had written 'it'. By writing words children gradually become aware of direction and of each letter individually – recognition tasks on their own do not help a great deal in learning these points. A child learns by doing, and if writing is made interesting by allowing freedom of media and expression, then he will enjoy these repetitive tasks. Watch a young child mastering any skill and you will notice how often he will repeat the task just for the sheer enjoyment of knowing he has mastery over it.

50

The words from the common words series will be required constantly by the child later, when he is writing, so it is surely wise to help him get these under his belt. (Examples of common words can be found on page 77.) Even the very young child, once he has learnt some letters, will be able to learn one word per week or fortnight, but certainly no more. There is no need to hurry this stage. If the child learns – *really* learns – one word a week, then in his first year he will have mastered all the common words he is likely to need for many years to come. For example, one of the most popular phrases used by young school children is 'I went to the. . .' This is required by them to write about their news. Now, if they learnt one of these words each week, soon the teacher would find her load greatly lightened.

Test the children regularly on their common words so that they come to regard spelling tests as easy stuff – something that is so easy they always get them right. Do not make the mistake of thinking that spelling tests are only for new words. Instead, test them regularly on the words they know, as it will reinforce their learning, and show them that spelling is enjoyable because there is no fear of failure. If the teacher has not rushed into teaching too many words when the child was not familiar with the earlier stages, then the child is bound to succeed. The teacher's aim should be one which stimulates success. It is better for a child to get three words right every time than to get thirteen words spelt wrongly most of the time. There are, of course, thousands and thousands of words which the child cannot spell but he should not be too aware of this in the early stages. He is building up confidence in spelling and this is of prime importance.

Postman and Bruner found in 1948 that if people are put in a stressful situation they are apparently unable to concentrate upon simple tasks requiring detailed visual perception. This surely also applies to children. Most poor spellers feel very inferior because of their inability to spell, and young school children often confess they 'hate' spelling. It is not just dislike or boredom – the spelling situation is one charged with emotion for them. Under these conditions they are most likely to find it even more difficult to relax and pay attention to the task in hand. Therefore, the teacher should avoid causing such an emotional upheaval. Take things slowly and make certain that each stage meets with success.

Coding System or Ordering

It is about this time that the child can start to become familiar with the coding system. It will be remembered that this is the way certain letters are grouped together in English and that each language has its own particular way of grouping letters. If the learner is familiar with letter groups, then these are learnt and recognised in 'chunks', thus making the spelling task easier. Sometimes there are only two letters in these chunks, although three- and four-letter groups are also common. The more proficient the speller becomes, the larger are the chunks he is able to memorise.

For the very young child, 'th' and 'sh' are useful starters since it is likely that he will meet these letter groups in his reading or common words. However, other groups could be 'an', 'on' and 'is', which also happen to be words, although in this case it is best to consider them simply as letters which often come together.

A task which is child-centred and therefore adapts to the learning capacity and background of the learner is 'hunt the group'. (This, as the name implies, is similar to the 'letter hunt' described on page 48.) A letter group is chosen for the week's 'hunt', and the children have to collect as many words as they can containing that letter group. These can be written by the children on a large blackboard, perhaps with the finder's initials alongside his particular find. There is no need to keep a permanent record of the words, nor do the children have to learn them which would spoil half the fun. The idea is to get children looking at words intently, to develop the habit of studying the internal structure of words.

A word of warning should be given to the teacher who sees this as a phonic exercise, for it is not that. It is building up visual awareness. Would a teacher who relies upon phonics allow *one* to be included in the 'on' list, or *pithead* in the 'th' list? These words would be included because they contain the correct visual pattern. Spelling is primarily about learning correct visual patterning and should not rely too heavily upon phonic cues. This 'hunt' encourages children to examine words for visual patterns.

Some teachers feel that the matter cannot be left simply at the hunting stage, but why not? If the children have shown an interest in words and their components then the task is complete. When looking at a new word it is likely that they will recognise familiar letter groups. For example, the child might spot the 'on' group in a word. Whilst this might not help in reading the word, which might be *action*, nevertheless if the child has to *write* the word then it is likely he will remember the 'on' as a chunk he has met before. In his written work he is therefore more likely to write *action* than *actoin*.

Gradually as the child becomes more and more familiar with letter groups, he will be able to recognise larger and larger chunks at a glance. Good spellers seem to require only one quick glance and a new word is learnt, but this has nothing to do with keen eyesight, rather that they are able to recognise visual chunks. How some very young children learn this on their own is still a mystery, for some children definitely acquire this skill at a very early age. However, as outlined above, others can be helped to acquire knowledge about the coding system, and the sooner they acquire this knowledge, the easier they will find the spelling task.

This then concludes the First Stage. The emphasis has been upon motor activities with the children learning letters; simple, everyday words they require in their writing, and an introduction has been made to the coding system. This motor learning should be treated as fun, with the teacher using all her ingenuity to encourage the children to practise writing. More than anything else, she should be fostering a positive attitude towards writing, for in spelling the child has to be an active learner.

6 Middle Stage

There is no exact cut-off point between each stage, for writing is a continuous activity, one skill merging very much into another. However, if the child has received ample opportunity to explore the pre-spelling or First Stage then he should have good groundwork and this Middle Stage will be easy. If the earlier groundwork is still faulty, the teacher should devise more activities to encourage the child in his motor skills. He will not progress if he is unsure about letters, simple words or has not made a start on recognising letter groups. The reader is referred in this case to the section on remedial teaching (Chapter Nine), which suggests new activities covering old ground.

We will however proceed, assuming the learner has a good knowledge of the following:

1. Can write from memory most commonly used letters. Knows them both in capital and lower case. Is able to supply at least one label for each letter, either the alphabetical name or sound.
2. Can write some of the common word series with confidence. The actual number of words will depend upon the child's age and background and it is left to the teacher to decide whether the child shows he understands that these are words he can use in his writing.
3. Is able to recognise some small letter groups and is able to play *hunt the group*.

There are no tests to determine whether a child has the necessary groundwork to proceed. Teaching is an art and the teacher will largely know when the child shows he is ready to proceed. However, (3) above can be tested by supplying the child with a number of word cards which he has to sort into 'sets'. How he divides them into sets will indicate his knowledge of the coding system. Do not criticise if he sees different sets to the ones you planned; he should in fact be encouraged to see how many different sets he can divide them into. For example, he may place *he*, *head* and *help* together having used the 'he' connection. You may have wanted him to group *he* with *me* and *be*; *head* with *bean* and *eat* and so on, but his groupings were equally as good as yours. Allow the child to show his own methods (you may be surprised how good his reasoning is) as this creates a positive attitude in the learner.

This Middle Stage is largely one of consolidating the familiarisation stage with its heavy dependence upon motors skills, and of gradually progressing towards the recognition stage with its reliance upon visual perception.

Letters

Now is the time to start teaching handwriting. Encourage clear writing whether the child adopts your style of writing or not. Show the children the most economical way of writing each letter. There are many excellent books on handwriting, so the matter will not be discussed here in detail. But don't suddenly change from a teacher who allows the children to write freely on their blackboards to one who insists on every fine point of letter production. Praise will make even the most slovenly writer take pains to improve. There is always something you can find to praise in handwriting, even if it is only the effort! Work towards a gradual improvement, and do not expect some miraculous change. That will never come. Instead, all the good work spent in the pre-spelling stage will evaporate, leaving the class feeling dejected and failures.

Handwriting requires a good deal of regular practice but it can be enjoyable for the children, especially if you allow them to write in coloured pencils or pen. Children usually like things to look 'nice' and grey pencils do not encourage them to take a pride in the appearance of their work. If you find the idea of coloured writing too gaudy, then let them write the title and date in colour, or the margin and underlining can be in colour. Whatever you use, try to develop this pride in the appearance of their work. Do not insist on rigid standards which add nothing to the total writing process except to make it boring.

At this stage of handwriting you will find left-handed children writing in peculiar postures. From my own experiences of watching left-handed writers I have been amazed at their skill in overcoming the problem in that when they write they tend to cover up what they have written, that is their writing hand hides the words they have just written. A right-handed person does not have this problem since we write left to right and all the work is visible, but not so with the left-handed person. Their papers and pens are often

When a left-hand writer persists in writing from right to left, draw a line down the left hand side of the paper. Every time the child writes he must first place his pencil on the guide line; since he cannot write towards the left he must now write in the left to right direction.

positioned so that they are able to see what they have written. Therefore, be wary of correcting left-handed writers, for their position suits their way of writing.

Should you find that some children are still writing in a right to left direction now is the time to correct it. Draw a line down the very edge of the left-hand side of the paper. The child is told to put his pencil *always* against that line and then start writing. Since the line is on the left, he has no option but to proceed across to the right. Continue with this method for all work until you feel he has developed the correct habit. There is seldom any point in trying to explain to a young learner that he must write in a left to right direction, or to make a fuss about which is left and which is right. Writing from the guide line develops the correct habit without confusing the child or making him feel that he is in any way different from the other children.

Common Word Series

By now the child should have a supply of words at his fingertips. If he possesses about ten known words, then he can take part in the following activity. It may still be necessary to test these words occasionally but now the learner should be encouraged to think of them as useful for writing, not simply words spelt in isolation. (Of course, it is hoped that he already uses most of the words in his small writing tasks, but the following activity reinforces the idea that words can be grouped into whole thought units.)

The child is given the word cards he knows how to spell. He arranges these words into a little phrase or sentence which is then copied on to a slip of paper. The teacher now tests him on the whole phrase or sentence. Say the whole phrase clearly, in a normal voice and at an ordinary speed. Do not keep repeating it, as this will interfere with the child's concentration as he writes. The idea is for the child to hold the whole phrase in his head and then write from memory. At the first attempt the child is likely to get stuck so let him finish writing as much as he can, then repeat the whole phrase again just as before. Continue until he is able to complete the whole phrase. Hand the slip of paper back to the child and allow him to mark his own work. Always encourage children to mark their own work since this encourages the checking habit. This work can also be conducted in small groups with each child taking it in turns to be 'teacher'.

Although this is a simple activity it does seem to have many advantages over the conventional dictation type task. First, the child already knows all the words so he is free to concentrate upon the meaning. Second, the phrase or sentence was composed by him therefore ensuring that as far as possible it reflects his style of speech. Third, since he composed it, it should make sense to him, which makes it easier for him to remember the whole group of words. Fourth, it introduces him to the idea that in free writing he works from meaning to print without being too conscious of each individual letter and word.

More Common Words

The child should continue to learn new common words, but again there should be no rush to learn a lot at each session. As before the aim should be to learn the most useful ones *thoroughly*. One per week is probably all that is required but the child should learn it so thoroughly that he never in his entire life falters on that word again.

The earlier activities which encouraged the child to write the word many times on his blackboard or in sand and so on will probably now seem inappropriate. By now the child should also have discarded the copying stage, since he now knows all the letters and some of the more common letter groups. The following activity is designed to develop the habit of looking carefully at new words and then writing them from memory.

Flap-cards

A new word is presented on a card but stapled to the front is a piece of fabric, which hides the word. The child lifts the fabric flap, reads the word, examines it carefully, drops the flap and then tries to write the word. If he gets stuck he has another quick peep and continues writing. Gradually, with practice, he should be able to write the whole word with one quick glance. If he makes a mistake he should not alter the word, but instead, write out the whole word again from memory.

The activity should be practised occasionally throughout the week so that by the end of the week the child is able to say, 'I don't need the card; I can write the word without looking.' This is excellent. If

Flap card

1   Flap card

2   Child lifts the flap and studies the word

3   Child writing from memory

4   Child checking his own attempt

the child is unable to do this by the end of one week, do not reprimand him but check with yourself that you have allowed him sufficient time at the groundwork stage and that he has not, in fact, been copying the previous words. If he has relied too heavily upon copying he will find this flap-card work very difficult so give him easy, short words to learn and slowly build up to more complicated ones. Whatever activity you use you must wean him away from the habit of copying.

The next two activities are recognition tasks and therefore should be used only after the children have learnt the words, not as a means of teaching them. Although earlier it was stated that reading should not be considered sufficient in itself to enable the learner to spell, nevertheless it seems from research that reading aloud may have some part to play in this, particularly if the words are read in isolation, that is, without any aid from context or pictures. The following games, which require children to read aloud words in isolation, seem to help in the teaching of spelling although the reasons for this are unknown.

Word Bingo

Word bingo is already used widely to teach reading and it is here suggested that the common words be used for this game. After learning a sufficient number of words, say ten, word bingo can be played as a revision exercise for these words. The children themselves take it in turns to be 'caller' so that each child has to read a word aloud at least once, and as the children are often quite happy to play this game at least three times a week they usually get plenty of practice in seeing the word and reading it aloud.

Pairs

This is another game which requires the children to read words aloud. Again take about ten words and provide two small cards for each word. All twenty cards are spread face downwards upon a table. The first child turns over two cards and calls out their words. If the words are a pair, i.e. the same, the child takes the pair of cards and has another turn. If the words are not a pair they are returned to their original positions and the next child has a go. The child with the most pairs when all cards have been taken (or the time runs out) is the winner.

Both these games require no help from the teacher, the rules are simple, the apparatus minimal, and perhaps more important than anything else – the children are working although they think of it as

59

playing. Once these games have been established in a class they can be played for years with the words becoming more and more complex. This also allows the teacher to have them all playing these games, but each group using words according to their own level, making it easier for classroom organisation.

Interest Words

Obviously, by now, the child will be requiring words not in the common word series and although the above activities can be used effectively it may mean that the teacher requires hundreds of cards to cover all the children's requirements.

It is now that we proceed one step further and require the child to examine a word and then decide upon the best way of remembering all the letters in their correct order. The child, however, must do the thinking; the teacher must not place him in a passive role where he has to rely upon her instruction.

Imagine a situation where the child is writing a sentence or two under his picture. He knows many of the common words so these do not present any problem. Then he comes across a word he does not know, possibly never having seen it in print before. So he appeals to the teacher for help. What is she to do? Obviously she cannot sit down there and then and give him an individual spelling lesson, nor would the child want it for he simply wants a word quickly so that he can proceed with his own writing.

If this is the first time the teacher has encountered this type of request from that child the simplest thing to do is to write the correct spelling on a slip of paper and allow him to copy it into his work. Do not impede his flow of writing, *but* at the very next opportunity make certain that the child, plus any others who are ready for word-building, are given some strategies to enable them to tackle new words. Sometimes this is the whole class, but whoever you select they must have covered the groundwork described in the First Stage, otherwise the following will be confusing rather than helpful.

Word Building

Get the group comfortably seated around a blackboard. Give the children a simple word, not in the common word series, but perhaps one which they will require in their topic work. Say the topic is one about pets so we shall use that word as the example. Ask for a volunteer to write the first letter, then another volunteer to write the second letter and so on. After the final letter ask the children whether you need any more volunteers or whether the word is complete. A child should be encouraged to judge whether a word is finished or not. Sometimes there is a silent letter or one which is barely audible. Never reprimand a child if his letter is incorrect, simply rub it out quickly and ask for another volunteer. Always encourage them to try. When the word is finished ask them to check the word by reading it to themselves and then to judge whether they think it looks right. This checking is a very important stage and can easily be taught so that it becomes a habit.

Ask the children for another word, perhaps again linked with their topic, but if not linked with topic work at least let it be a word they will need to use. Continue with the group trying to build up the word letter by letter and give as much praise as possible. In these early stages the children should feel that the task is easy, but of course sooner or later you will be given a word that is not phonically regular.

For example all might be going smoothly with *cat* and *dog* and *fish* then a child gives the word *gerbil*. What are you to do? This is where teaching skill comes into play, for there is no one answer. The teacher has to weigh up the situation and the children's knowledge of letters. Are they able to deal with the two sounds of 'g' in such words as *gave* and *giant*? Is there a gerbil in the classroom making it more important to know this word? Is there a label already on the cage which will aid in the work? The teacher's skill will enable her to proceed. Often the children appreciate honesty and if you admit that this word is going to be more tricky they usually like the challenge. At some time or other the children have to learn that not all words lend themselves to auditory analysis and the teacher will have to judge when and how this fact has to be learnt.

These word-building discussion groups should continue at regular intervals so that children develop the confidence to try new words. Gradually the children will acquire the ability to link similar words to aid them with word-building, but this must be treated with care otherwise they will think they can always apply this technique. For example, during the pets topic work they might want to spell the word *straw* and already know the word *draw*. Their attention can be drawn to the similarities as a spelling aid.

Through this type of discussion work the children will learn to use either auditory analysis or spelling patterns encountered in known words, or both methods. They should be encouraged to consider different alternatives, for sometimes one method works for one word and sometimes a different method works for another. The aim of the group work is to try and get the child attempting the word

61

on his own. This attitude is even more important than the word itself, for the child is developing the attitude that spelling is generally rational and can often be attempted with a fair measure of success. However, our language is such that we can never be certain of a spelling of an unknown word until it has been checked. How is a young child to check his attempt? The following considers some of the simplest, and yet often overlooked, resources within the classroom.

Using Resources

Few people know how to spell every word they require but they are not troubled by this fact for they are able to consult other sources to check the spelling. One obviously first thinks of the dictionary but there are other sources and the child should be made aware of these.

Most of these resources are a matter of common sense but sometimes the emphasis has been so strongly upon actually *knowing* the correct spelling that the child feels he is cheating if he uses some other source.

The most obvious source is the teacher or some other adult. When a child wishes to know how to spell a word he requires for his writing he is often instructed to bring his personal dictionary open at the correct page to the teacher, so that she can write in the required word. This encourages the child to analyse the word up to the first sound but is this really enough? Should the child be taught that provided he can analyse the first sound correctly, the teacher will supply all the rest of the word without any more effort on his part?

Once the children have done some word-building as outlined above, they should be encouraged to bring to the teacher their attempt at the whole word. The attempt can be written on slips of rough paper or small blackboards about twelve inches by four inches. Sometimes children prefer working on these small blackboards since their attempts are not permanent and they feel free to experiment. The child tries to write the word using either auditory analysis or similarity with known words, or a bit of both. He shows it to the teacher who should praise all attempts, especially in the early stages. It is most likely to be wrong, but not entirely wrong, so she should be able to praise something. The correct spelling is written underneath the child's attempt so that he can compare the closeness of his attempt. He then returns to his seat and copies the word into his free writing.

He is *not* required to learn the word. Children soon learn not to attempt difficult words if they are required to learn them for testing at some later date! The learning situation was involved in the actual word-building, and should the child require the word again on another day, he will again be required to build up the word, which will probably be easier this time. However, the child may use his natural cunning and refer to his earlier work and copy the word straight into his work. This latter policy should by no means be frowned upon by the teacher, for this independent spirit in the child to seek out the correct spelling is something we are trying to encourage.

As the children become more proficient the teacher will find that her role becomes one of checker, and at the same time the children become more confident in their own ability to get many spellings right first time. Of course, this situation is not easy to achieve, and one of the main problems is the teacher's authoritative role. The child should feel free to come to an adult and ask, 'Is this how you spell . . .?' without feeling he is going to be lectured or ridiculed if he is wrong. Insist on some attempt at the spelling, and provided the teacher does not make the child feel embarrassed about any error, he will continue coming to her for help *and* attempting the word himself. It is most important that the child tries to spell it on his own in the first instance. Later when the child wishes to consult a dictionary he will still need to make some attempt first, otherwise he has little idea of where to look for the particular word. Therefore, always encourage an attempt.

The idea of asking another for the correct spelling is sensible and encourages the children to co-operate with each other rather than being competitive. If a child is writing about going to another child's party but is uncertain how to spell that child's name, the obvious thing to do is to ask the child. Children should be aware that often names are spelt in a very personal way and even an adult often has to check. In this case the teacher would not be required for she is not the authority. Instead the child is the authority, for he knows how to spell his own name.

The classroom is often full of resources and the children should be helped to see them all around them. When I asked my son how he was managing to spell the names of various dinosaurs he told me he asked a friend. I was rather surprised as the friend was not known for his good spelling. It was then pointed out that this friend posses-sed a book on dinosaurs which he proudly consulted whenever he was asked for help. The children had solved a spelling problem on their own and this is always good. By all means use the teacher, but the children must learn to use other reliable resources as well.

When a group or class is studying a project it is likely they will all require similar words. They themselves can be asked for suggested words, which can be built up with their co-operation just as in the discussion work described earlier. The children arrange these words in alphabetical order, with the help of an alphabet if they are still unsure of the order, and then write the words out neatly, and display them for other children's use. This writing task has a definite purpose and the children will perform it responsibly, taking care the words are copied correctly and neatly, otherwise the other children will soon voice their complaints. This list can be consulted by other pupils before they go to the teacher to check on a spelling, and the teacher is made redundant for many words. At the same time the children become more independent in their search for the correct spelling.

So far this is only an introduction to the use of resources for checking spellings. Dictionaries and other resources will be developed further in the Final Stage of learning to spell.

Coding System

So far the child has become aware of letter pairs and simple common letter groups. By now he should feel confident enough to try longer letter groupings and be encouraged to think of his own spelling patterns. For example, the 'hunt' could be to look for words with double letters, such as *spelling, letter, school, Leeds*, or words with the pattern 'same-change-same' in words such as *complete, sincere, Oxo, these, cycle*.

This is not teaching them a way of learning the words, but simply getting them familiar with letter groupings so that when they are eventually looking at a new word with a view to remembering it, they will be able to say, 'Hello, thingummybob again!' Being familiar with a letter grouping aids recognition and recall. The learner looks at a new word with the intention of analysing it into meaningful parts, therefore the more familiar he is with different sorts of groupings the more efficient will be his analysis.

With some letter groups, such as 'ing', 'ful', 'ment' and 'ly' there is a temptation to embark on spelling rules. These will, however, be unnecessary, for the child requires the word as an example of a letter group and is not interested in why some other letters have been omitted or not as the case may be. The child himself, will most likely notice that in the example of 'ing' some words do not have the final 'e' as he expected, such as *having* and *coming*. If he has noticed this then all well and good, there is no need to evoke the spelling rule; if he has not spotted this connection then he is not ready for the generalisation and the spelling rule may confuse him – it will certainly deny him the opportunity of deducing it for himself and this is half the fun of learning.

As the children become more and more experienced hunters the teacher can impose some restrictions just to make it more difficult and challenging. She can ask for words with 'ing' in the middle such as *singer*, or words containing 'ed' anywhere but at the end, or unusual letter pairs such as 'sy' and 'rh' at the beginning.

Another form of hunt which acts as revision is the 'baton race'. One group starts by providing say five words with a common letter group such as 'er'. They display their words on the class noticeboard, then give a copy to the next group who have to add another five words also containing the 'er' pair. The procedure is the same for this group, who pass it on to the next, and so on. The whole race can take a week or longer with the best spellers left until last, which makes their task more difficult since no word can be duplicated. Sometimes another class can be prevailed upon to take up the 'baton' and continue adding 'er' words. At the end of the race all words can be placed in alphabetical order and displayed for the children's attention. Even those who find these 'hunts' difficult can thus feel pride in having been part of a really big 'hunt'.

Examples of children's 'Letter Group Hunts'

Both children were nearly nine years old. They did not attend the same school. The first, a boy, had considerable practice as his teacher set weekly 'Letter Group Hunts' for all children in the class. The work was all his own.

1. Words beginning with 'sy'

Sydney	sympathy	synagogue
sycamore	sympathetic	syrup
symbol	symphony	system

2. Words beginning with 'th'

the	through	then
they	thunder	them
thought	thirst	themselves
throw	thumb	thermostat
their	thistle	thermometer
there	thrush	these
those	throat	thief
thou	thigh	thieves

thick	thin	thimble
think	than	thorn
three	thing	thread
thirty	that	threaten
thirteen	thank	throne
thirsty	thaw	Thursday
throng	theatre	threw

The second child, a girl, had very little practice in 'Letter Group Hunts' but nevertheless, with a little aid from an older sister managed to complete the following 'hunt'. Although she had received some help she could read all the words and knew their meanings.

3. Words containing 'tion'

mention	attraction	condition
subtraction	auction	alteration
station	audition	nation
function	description	destruction
action	vibration	congratulation
inspection	addition	congregation
correction	multiplication	motion
direction	attention	detention

Summary of the Middle Stage

This Middle Stage has been a consolidation of the groundwork described in the Pre-Spelling/First Stage, as well as an introduction to the spelling process. Gradually the familiarisation stage is being left behind and more of the task involves recognition skills. However, since the children are now writing more they are still using the motor skills which are so important in the process of learning to spell. It must always be borne in mind that spelling is essential only for writing, and the ability to write freely must be the ultimate goal.

In this Middle Stage the children have been learning a clear and efficient style of handwriting, and ways of learning how to spell new words, discovering more complex letter groupings, and having an introduction to the use of resources to help check spellings. All these aspects help the child to write more freely.

7 Final Stage

It has already been established that each section blends in with the previous one. However, before commencing the final section it is worth considering whether the child has mastered the following:

1. The child should have an efficient style of writing which above all is clear to read. The style of writing can be print or cursive, but it must be clear. Possibly children should not be encouraged too early to abandon printing. It may seem grown-up to use the cursive style, but even adults use printing when they want to be certain of clarity.
2. The child should know how to spell at least 100 most common words. The spelling of these words should not be at the conscious level – he should be able to write them so fluently that his mind is not on the words but rather the meaning he wishes to convey. He should be able to write in short phrases rather than just individual words, although the latter is necessary at times.
3. The child should be developing various strategies for word-building and know how to check these against some 'authority', which might be a teacher, another pupil, or a word list. By using a word list the child understands the importance of alphabetical order.
4. The child should now be familiar with most common letter groups, i.e. possess knowledge of the basic coding system used in English, so that at a glance he is able to recognise and remember chunks when studying new words.

As with the earlier stages, the teacher should beware of hurrying the learner too fast through each activity. However, if the earlier stages have been carried out at the child's pace, not too fast and not too slow, and the children are not confused or bored, the Final Stage will be completed rapidly.

This Final stage develops (3) and (4). An occasional practice of (1) and (2) is all that is required, for by now the child should have thoroughly mastered these two areas.

Word-building

The discussion work carried out in the Middle Stage should be continued with a slight variation as follows.

While it is useful being able to build words directly from language, this is not the most common spelling problem. We usually know *roughly* what the word looks like from our reading, but we need some way of remembering all the letters in their correct order. In other words, we are not limited only to the sounds of the word – we have seen it perhaps many times before but now need some way of fixing the visual image. Until a child is reading fairly fluently he will not need this practice because (a) he has not encountered many difficult words and (b) the common words he meets in his reading he already knows how to spell.

Consider the situation where we have a discussion group ready to learn the word *difficult*. As a first attempt they could use volunteers to build up the word from the sound only, and it is likely they will produce quite a good attempt. But let us imagine that they have produced *dificult*, which the teacher corrects by writing underneath the correct word *difficult*. First, let them spot the difference which is giving them another opportunity for checking.

The teacher then erases their attempt and the children examine the correct spelling. The problem facing them now is to say how they, personally, would try and remember the correct spelling. They should be encouraged to think of this as requiring an individual solution. There is no 'best' way; each child should use his own particular solution for that particular word and the teacher should show interest in all answers.

For example, one child might say, 'The word is written how it sounds but I have to remember that there are two "f"s. Another child might say, 'There is a same-change-same pattern of "iffi" then the word "cult"'. Whilst another might suggest 'I divide it into three parts: "dif", "fi" and "cult"'. It really does not matter too much what they say provided it shows they are trying to analyse the word into meaningful parts. The word is then covered over and the children try to write the word from memory, thus testing whether their method worked for that particular word.

A trick which often works with young children is to tell them to think of their eyes as a camera; they are to 'take a picture' of the word and when the word is no longer in front of them they have to reproduce (write it) from the picture in their mind. The task of reproducing the word after it has been removed from sight has already been practised in the flap-card activity, so the children are familiar with the task. However, these longer, more complex words require the child to analyse the word in a way meaningful to him.

In order to remember these words the children will be using their coding knowledge. Take the word *knowledge*; some might immediately spot the 'kn' and 'dg' groups which will make their recall of these parts slightly easier. If they then remember that the 'kn' was found in the word *know* and 'dg' was in the word *ledge* or *edge*, then the word will present very little difficulty for them. Even if they are able to recognise only the letter pairs at least they are unlikely to make errors at these parts and can then concentrate upon analysing the rest of the word. The more familiar they are with the coding system, the more likely they are to be able to recognise chunks which are already known and do not have to be learnt again.

As in the word-building carried out in the Middle Stage they should be encouraged to consider each word afresh, weighing up the best way of analysing and remembering it, rather than thinking of one strategy which will fit all words. They are, in fact, developing the skill of examining each word as efficiently as possible.

Although the task requires visual perception the motor skill needed for writing the word should also be employed. A simple way of allowing the children to check their own attempts and give them practice in writing the word is to let them write the set word from memory on the top line of a long strip of paper. This word is checked against the correct spelling, then the word is folded over and the word again written from memory. Again the word is checked, then folded and written again, and so on until the child can write the word quickly, confidently and correctly. This folded strip of paper can be used again later in the week, with the child again checking his own attempts. The child can also take these folded strips of paper home to learn any spellings, which is far better than sending a child home with a list of words to be learnt by the end of the week, with no activities to help him learn the words.

Although the words are more difficult and more complex now they should not be outside the child's requirements. There is little point in spending time examining a word which the child neither knows how to pronounce, nor understands its meaning, nor has any need for in his writing. We learn spellings in order to make writing easier for both writer and reader. There are so many words the children want to learn to spell it seems pointless wasting time on obscure words or even pseudo-words. Practice for no purpose makes no sense. The purpose should always be for use in writing.

Folded strip

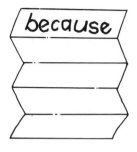

1 Word is copied onto the top fold

2 Paper is folded over and the child writes from memory

3 Child checks his own attempt

Resources

The children should already be familiar with the idea of checking spellings against a reliable source. So far the sources have been immediate, such as the teacher, other pupils, or a class word list devised for a particular project. It will be remembered that this list was arranged alphabetically, and the practice children received in using this sort of list will help in the more advanced search activities considered now.

One of the best resources to check spellings is by using the dictionary, but often teachers do not realise how difficult a dictionary search is for a child. They expect one lesson arranging a list of words in alphabetical order to be all that is required for success with a dictionary. Also, many textbooks give dictionary exercises which

70

consist of looking up words in order to slot the correct one into incomplete sentences. Most people consult dictionaries not for the meaning of words but to check a spelling. Therefore the dictionary exercise as described above is artificial for a child. At a later stage in their education they might require a dictionary to compare the different nuances of meaning of two or three words, but this is seldom their first concern. Most children use a dictionary to check spellings, so this purpose will be foremost in the activities.

Learning to Use a Dictionary

Spellings are usually checked when a person is actually in the process of writing. They have to stop their writing and their main concern is to find the spelling quickly so that they can return to their writing. Therefore speed is an important factor when considering how to teach a child how to use a dictionary.

Stage 1: Alphabetical Order

1. On a long thin strip of paper or card the children write out the alphabet as neatly as possible. This is going to be their check card for the following games so they must get the order correct. It is often best for the children to work in groups building up the alphabet; it might take a little longer for them all to agree the correct order but it is to be preferred to the teacher simply handing out cards carrying the alphabet. If the children cannot agree or need help, give them a dictionary and let them work through it finding each letter in turn. Do not hurry this stage, for the rest of the work depends upon this foundation.
2. Now give the children an envelope containing perhaps ten little cards, each showing one letter. They do not look at these yet.
3. In their jotters they number down one to ten. Now they are ready to start.
4. Taking it in turns a child takes one card from the envelope, calls out the letter, puts the card face upwards on the table, says 'go' then they all have to find any word in the dictionary starting with that letter. The word is written in their jotters. When looking for a letter in the dictionary the child might forget the precise position of that letter within the alphabet so he refers to his alphabet check card.
5. The first child to find a word beginning with the set letter is awarded three marks, the second gets two marks and the third gets one mark. It is the first child to *find* the word (not write it) who gains the marks; the word can then be written carefully and correctly while the other children are still trying to find a word. If

there are any arguments or cheating, the caller can miss his turn and be 'teacher' for that particular letter.

There are many advantages of this method over the exercise whereby the child has to place words into alphabetical order. The main advantages are listed below:

1. The child is learning the correct alphabetical order by an activity which concentrates upon only one letter at a time. The order is seen to be meaningful to the child.
2. The child is becoming familiar with handling a dictionary.
3. Very little equipment is needed, and it can be used time and time again. The task is simple yet the children are active.
4. The work can be done either individually, in pairs, in small groups or the whole class can be occupied. Children who work quickly can work together and the slower ones can also work together. In this activity this does not always relate to academic ability.
5. The activity can be easily extended to contain pairs of letters or longer letter groupings, and this aids spelling as well as teaching the child to use a dictionary. This further activity should be attempted only when the children are truly skilled at finding first letters. Examples of useful letter pairs are: 'qu', 'kn', and 'th' and so on, whilst 'squ', 'pre' and 'com' are examples of useful longer groupings.

Stage 2

Returning to the idea of why we consult a dictionary it will be remembered that first it had to be a quick operation and second we needed to look up unknown words. So far the child has learnt to use a dictionary at speed using a visual cue – cards. Any word would suffice provided it had the correct starting letters, but in real life we are usually working from auditory cues, so this skill must be catered for.

The following game is identical to the one used in the First Stage except that the caller reads out a *word* shown on the card, and does not show the other players the card until the word has been found in the dictionary. The scoring can be the same and, as before, the children take it in turns to be the caller.

At this stage we are not attempting to widen their vocabulary or make the task difficult, so keep the words well within their knowledge with no trick starts – this comes later. The words can be linked to their other class work which makes the dictionary game even more purposeful.

Where possible it is usually best to start with simple sounding words, for after all, we are asking the children to use auditory analysis and this is not made easy if the word starts with something like 'phy' or 'psu'.

The players are also getting practice in reading with care, for there will be an uproar from the others if they mis-read the card. As mentioned earlier, reading words in isolation seems to aid spelling, perhaps because the reader has to examine every part of the word before he commits himself to saying what he thinks it is. A rough guess is just not good enough for this game and the others will let him know it.

If it is necessary to do this work individually then a tape recorder can be used to 'call' out the words. However, make certain that the words are recorded in a normal voice with plenty of space between each word so that the child has time to switch off the machine without running into the next word. Trying to rewind and search for one particular word can be very irritating.

Stage 3

If Stages 1 and 2 have been worked through steadily, allowing the child to master each stage before progressing to the next, he will by now be pretty adept at using the dictionary and what is more will probably enjoy using it.

This stage is similar to the game used in the Second Stage, but now considers word endings. These are normally taught in the form of spelling rules, but most children find this next activity preferable for two reasons:

1. They can make the inferences themselves.
2. They learn that the dictionary can assist with endings. Mistakes are often made when adding suffixes and any future uncertainty can be checked by reference to a good dictionary; they do not have to try and remember rules.

For this activity allow the children to use really large dictionaries, partly because endings are not always contained in simplified versions and also because children feel very grand being allowed to use 'grown-up' dictionaries.

The words recorded now cover, for instance, plural endings. Again take it easy with simple 's' and 'es' to commence with. At another session 'ys' and 'ies' can be dealt with. Then perhaps a combination of the two, with the children making their own attempts first, then using the dictionary to check. Other suggested endings are: 'ing', 'tion', 'ful', 'ly', 'ness', 'ence', 'ance'.

Another variation on the above game is to give the children trick starts, such as 'gn' in *gnome*, 'kn' in *knight*, 'pn' in *pneumonia*. All the words sound as though they begin with 'n' but none of them do. A good idea is to include the simple 'n' start as well, otherwise children will anticipate difficult beginnings without realising that the simple one is the most common. However, as mentioned previously, do not try to teach it as some sort of rule, but let the children play it as a game, and they will soon see the connection.

Other trick starts are:
'r' sound: 'wr' as in *write* and 'rh' as in *rhubarb*
's' sound: as in *cycle* and 'ps' as in *psalm*
'c' sound: as in *king* and *Christmas*

Summary

Of course, learning to spell does not finish once the children have completed these activities. They have been designed to help in the teaching of spelling, but as new, more complex words are encountered the learner will need to continue assimilating them into his written vocabulary. Learning to spell should continue throughout life and the above suggestions merely provide the groundwork upon which this learning can take place.

However, the learner should now have an efficient style of handwriting, know at least 250 common words which he can write without hesitation, possess various strategies for learning new words, and know how to consult a dictionary or other resources when in doubt. The learner should now feel free to write, unhampered by hesitancy over spelling.

8 A Spelling Curriculum

As the word 'curriculum' can have a very wide usage, in this chapter it will be defined as subject curriculum, i.e. referring to the material to be taught in schools.

It is usual to find a definite curriculum in all subjects except spelling, and the reason seems to be that in the past too little attention has been paid to the learning process involved in spelling. In 1980 I was informed by the Schools Council that no spelling projects had been carried out to date and Uta Frith stated in 1980 'The study of spelling has only just started and many mysteries remain.' (*Cognitive Processes in Spelling* p. viii)

To the layman this seems incredible, for spelling is basic knowledge required for one of the three R's, yet in 1980 it was being considered a new subject! Having read this far, the reader will hopefully have some overall plan as to ways in which spelling can be learnt, for it is impossible to devise a spelling curriculum without knowledge of how spelling can be acquired. Each step and each activity should be part of the whole process, from the single letter to letter groups, to automatic retrieval of most common words and skill in finding the correct spelling when in doubt.

This does not mean that all the letters have to be learnt, and then all letter groups, and then words and so on in some rigidly constructed set of programmes. The skilled teacher requires expert knowledge of the whole spelling process so that she is able to utilise the opportunities which present themselves, and foster an atmosphere conducive to good spelling. That is, the teacher will neither be restricted by an imposed programme of instruction, nor wait for some sort of 'happening' to occur so that she can embark upon the teaching of spelling. She will use her expertise to make suitable situations as well as be alert to the way she can use the unexpected events which occur in all classes throughout most of the day. This is why it is difficult to suggest how to conduct even one spelling lesson, let alone a whole school curriculum. However, guidelines can be suggested and it is the school's responsibility to modify them according to their own requirements.

There are two levels operating at the same time and it is important to realise that they do not both have to conform to the same requirements. The contact level, where the teacher is presenting the material to the children, is flexible and depends upon her own teaching style and the needs of the class. The curriculum level is an overall plan which allows the teacher to know how much she is required to teach to her children. This curriculum should ideally be the result of detailed discussion with all the teachers, and its effectiveness in covering all necessary steps should be reconsidered at least annually. It should be fairly rigid and subject to alteration only after consultation with other teachers. As defined in this book the curriculum is concerned with subject knowledge, but it should be left to the teacher to select the appropriate methods.

The age of the children and the composition of the school will naturally affect it, but since most of the skills required for spelling are learnt during the early years of schooling, more attention will be given to the curriculum of the first or primary school. However, the divisions are arbitrary, and the suggestions which follow are intended only as guidelines.

Five to Seven Years

The work described in the First Stage (Chapter Five) should be tackled during these years. However, children will be developing at their own rate and it is suggested that teachers work closely together so that (a) the teachers are aware of the experiences the children have had before they joined her class, (b) apparatus and words are not duplicated unnecessarily and (c) the teachers do not feel that they are restricted by an over-ambitious syllabus. The following are suggestions for each year, though in practice, the brighter children will complete more each year and there is no good reason for holding them back. Nor is there any point in trying to push the slower learner. If we try to hurry him through the work before he is ready for it, it will only confuse him and certainly not improve his spelling performance.

Letter Familiarisation

This is the main activity for these years and for each letter studied the child should be able to:
1. copy the letter
2. 'write' or reproduce it from memory

3. name the letter
4. recognise the letter in various sizes and forms, e.g. T t *T t*.

Common Words

These can be learnt alongside the learning of letters as above. In the first year the child might learn:

> his name, his road
> I, went, to, my, it, is, the, in, and, of (*10 words*)

Second year:

> name of some close relation, such as brother, sister or friend, or his town
> a, he, that, was, at, be, are, for, have, his, not, on, said, so, they, we, with, you, she, can (*20 words*)

Towards the end of the second year, the child will be able to compose short sentences or phrases from his known words and have these dictated for him to check. Examples are as follows:

> 'I went to', 'it is in', 'and it is'
> 'she went to', 'he is in', 'they said so'

Coding System

An introduction to phonic work as well as a coding system can be made by hunting for words containing phonic pairs such as:
First year: sh, ch, th, qu, st
Second year: bl, br, pl, pr, er, ing

Attitude

Although left until last, this item is probably the most important particularly for slow learners. Even if the child has not been able to learn any letters he should not have any reason to consider himself a failure. The teacher of young children should be fostering a willingness to write, even if it is still at the blackboard and sand tray stage. The children should leave these classes with a feeling of their own competence in writing even if it is only at the 'copy writing' stage. If the teacher has taught the children all the above work but they loathe writing then she has definitely failed in her task.

Eight to Ten Years

For most children this is the time when they need to expand their writing from small sentences describing simple straightforward events to complicated sentences which cover all manner of subject matter in varying styles. It will be appreciated that in order to make such a large step, from mere labelling to actual writing, the ground-work must be firmly established. The wise teacher will be able to devise new activities to stimulate the slow learners so that they continue with the work described in the five to seven year old section without feeling they are just repeating old work. Suggestions are contained in the chapter on remedial teaching. It is most important that all children develop the framework on which the next work will depend, otherwise they will become confused and dejected, and forget even the work which they apparently could manage with ease.

Letters

Neat and efficient handwriting is now emphasised with the child developing a personal pride in the display and layout of his work.

Common words

Third year: all, as, but, had, him, an, been, by, came, from, got,
(7–8 years) has, her, here, if, like, made, me, my, new, now, our, out, see, some, them, there, this, when, which
(30 words)

Fourth about, back, before, call, come, could, did, do, down,
year: first, get, go, into, just, little, look, make, more, much,
(8–9 years) must, no, off, only, or, over, other, right, their, then, up, want, well, who, were, what, where, will, your, would, yes (40 words)

Fifth year: after, again, always, ask, any, because, bring, book,
(9–10 years) every, found, friend, gave, give, good, how, jump, keep, know, last, left, live, long, many, never, next, nothing, once, open, own, play, put, ran, read, road, room, round, saw, say, school, should, sing, soon, stop, street, take, tell, than, these, thing, think, time, too, under, very, walk, water, why, wish, work, would
(60 words)

These words are chosen for their need in the written work of young children, not according to a reading scheme or their degree of difficulty. Most children use the past tense when writing, therefore, these are often placed before the present tense. Also children seldom use questions in their early writing, so that question-type words have also been left till later.

Useful Words

Besides the common word series there are many useful words which it is as well to learn early on. These are often proper nouns so that the children can learn the purpose of capital letters incidentally when they learn the words.

Third year: Monday, Tuesday, Wednesday, Thursday, Friday,
(*7–8 years*) Saturday, Sunday
          day, days, week, and some basic colours such as red,
          green, blue, yellow, white and black
Fourth   January, February, March, April, May, June, July,
year: August, September, October, November, December
(*8–9 years*) month, year, birthday, holiday
          Easter, Christmas, spring, summer, autumn, winter
Fifth year: one, two, three, four, five, six, seven, eight, nine, ten,
(*9–10 years*) twenty, hundred, thousand, million

These are only suggestions and the teacher may instead like to substitute or add extra words which she finds are frequently required in her children's writing. The teacher can collect these and then select the 'core' words which are needed most. As with the common words, keep the number of words to the minimum but make sure the children learn these words so thoroughly that they will never forget them. With such strict requirements obviously only the most essential words will appear in the syllabus. Keep the syllabus realistic and do not attempt too much. Too much time is wasted in schools in learning long lists of words which the children neither require nor even know. Possible twenty or thirty words a year is all that is required, even from the brightest child, though many children will learn more than this.

Resources

During the eight to ten year age range all children will be writing freely, perhaps with the exception of one or two children who are still working on the earlier sections. However, the majority will now be encountering words not learnt in their common word series, and so need to learn strategies to overcome these problem words.

Although individual dictionaries are popular in most schools they are seldom more than a place where the teacher writes the problem word. The child seldom thinks of checking his dictionary first to discover whether he had asked for that word earlier, and so it is possible to find the same word cropping up time and time again in the same book.

The personal dictionary should not, under any circumstances, contain any common words supposedly learnt in earlier years. The child must learn to rely upon his own memory. If he says he has forgotten how to spell a common word then this indicates he did not learn the word thoroughly in the first place. After all, we do not forget how to spell our own name, even though we may not require to write it for quite some time. When the child learns the common words he should learn each word with the thoroughness he applies to learning his name, that is, so he will *never* forget the correct spelling.

Chapter Six (Middle Stage) contains suggestions on how to supply words required by the child in his free writing, but gradually he will be moving on to using dictionaries and the teacher will have to use her own skill and judgement in deciding when to use the dictionary activities described in Chapter Seven. It is, therefore, difficult to subdivide this section into year groups since it depends so much upon the individual requirement of each child.

Throughout this section the teacher should be gradually weaning the child away from always asking her to check his spelling of a new word so that he learns independence. This will come gradually and requires confidence on the part of the learner to appreciate that he is able to find the word for himself from a variety of sources. The teacher must be on the lookout for opportunities to encourage the child to use his own ideas, appropriate for each word. For example, when checking the name of a country or city it is best to consult an atlas, but when the word is an author's name, a book written by that person is the best source, and so on.

The child will at some stage learn that not all adults know how to spell all words, and the teacher should be willing to admit when she is uncertain of a particular spelling. The teacher might have to ask a child how he spells his own name, or she might have to consult a textbook or dictionary for the spelling of a technical word. The teacher should not labour the point, but on the other hand neither should she try to disguise the fact that she does not know a spelling. Incidentally, the child will be learning how others set about the task of checking a spelling and they will realise that there is nothing childish about having to check words. Fear of looking ridiculous often inhibits the poor speller from asking or even consulting a dictionary, as if he was displaying his ignorance by needing to use another source. The teacher can help a great deal by building up a positive attitude towards using resources intelligently.

80

Coding System

By now the child will have a general knowledge about spelling which allows him to judge whether a word could be English or a nonsense word, although such knowledge would most likely be 'hidden'. That is, the child would be unable to explain why he thought a word was English or nonsense. The fact that the child instinctively recognises English-like words means that he is developing a coding system based upon familiar letter groups. It is now the teacher's task to develop this knowledge so that the child's coding system becomes larger and more flexible. The following is again only a suggested programme and although at first glance it might appear to be a phonic list, it should be remembered that this is based upon visual patterns and not auditory cues.

Third year: 'ar', 'ee', 'ou', 'in', 'tr', 'gl', 'gr', 'cr', 'cl' and double
(7–8 years) letters
           Example 1: 'In' found in words such as *thin* and *pin* but also *find*
           Example 2: for double letters *tree*, *Daddy* and *shopping* would all be in the same list

Fourth 'ow', 'ea', 'ck', 'or', 'ed', 're', words ending in 'y', words
year: ending in 'e', same-change-same pattern
(8–9 years) Example 1: 're' in *read*, *return*, *fire* and *are*
           Example 2: same-change-same in *here*, *sister*, *ewe*

Fifth year: 'kn', 'ph', 'ex', 'tion', 'ght', 'au', 'wh' and 'wr'
(9–10 years)

Throughout this time the child should be developing the habit of seeing words in chunks. The flap-card work, described in Chapter Six, and the word building discussion work described in Chapter Seven, afford opportunities for the child to use his coding knowledge.

Dictation

By the age of eight the child will have memorised sufficient words to be able to form small sentences or phrases for dictation practice. As the aim is simply to get him thinking and writing groups of words effortlessly, keep the length of dictation very short. There is no need for this to be reserved for test work, but rather let the child dictate one small sentence to his own group each day. As mentioned before, the whole phrase or sentence should be given in one go, so that the child acquires the skill of holding a related passage in his mind while writing each word.

Examples from each age group will illustrate the brevity of the task, although these examples should not be 'given' to the children, since the whole idea is to get them to supply their own sentences or phrases.

Seven to eight: 'She came to see them.' 'They have got a new car.'
Eight to nine: 'Where did you go?' 'Who will see them?'
Nine to ten: 'I know it is February.' 'Should I walk to school?'

Writing

Towards the end of this age group some children will be ready for lessons in cursive script and it is suggested that word cards be made for them.

Thus by the time the child is ten +, he has an efficient style of handwriting which enables him to concentrate on the purpose of writing rather than on the mechanics of the task. This is not simply a pedantic requirement, for research has shown that children with a slow awkward way of writing are usually also poor spellers. The reasons for this are still uncertain, but it seems that if the mechanics of writing are difficult for the child then he will write less and consequently receive less practice in writing. Conversely, if he becomes a quick and clear writer he will probably write more, thus becoming more familiar with more words. He will most likely also *enjoy* writing, as we all enjoy practising skills in which we know we are proficient.

Therefore the teacher should not discourage a child from writing just because she feels the need to insist upon neatness, but rather gradually build up the child's pride in his own work and style.

Ten + Years

Letters

Obviously very little work will be required in this section except to encourage the children to develop an adult style of writing.

Common Words

Except for the slow learner, all children will have mastered the basic common words, and together with other useful words will now possess a basic core of over 200 words to aid them in their writing. Some revision may be necessary in the form of dictated phrases and sentences so that they are now easily able to hold a complete phrase in their heads while they continue to write. In other words, the children have approached the stage whereby common words are written automatically without hesitancy over which letter comes next.

Coding System

So far only some of the most common letter groups have been encountered in 'hunts', and whilst some of the younger children might still require help in identifying new letter groups, most will have developed the habit of looking for familiar chunks, and therefore there is no need to feel that they all have to work through all letter groups. Each child will now continue developing his own coding system, even though he might not be able to explain what he is doing, and so the work can now include derivations of words or unusual letter groups such as:

Ten to eleven years: 'un, 'dis', 'less', 'ful', 'ly', 'tri', 'bi', 'cent'
Eleven to twelve years: 'tele', 'ology', 'ical', 'mn' and beginnings of words such as 'rh' and 'sy'

Children in these years are often able to complete fantastic 'baton races' which allows them to display their skill with words and of course provides revision of earlier work. However, this should not be done too often, as the main aim should be fun.

Word-building

The child should now be developing flexible strategies for dealing with new words. This should be extremely easy for him especially as the work is based upon his knowledge of the English coding system.

Through group discussion the children should be studying words, asking themselves questions such as, 'Can this word be written as it is said?' 'How would I divide it into chunks?' 'Are there any parts which I think are tricky?' 'Is it like any word I already know?' 'Is it a compound word which I can divide into sections?' Each child must be confident to develop his own style of questioning, and accept that there is no ideal answer, just personal preference.

The motor skills should still be used to establish whether the learner's strategy was appropriate or not. As mentioned before, it is only by writing the word from memory that we really face the fact of whether we know the word or whether some letters are 'hazy'.

Gradually, the learner will find that it is unnecessary to check by writing. A concentrated study, even of only a few seconds, is all that is required by the competent speller. The word is analysed into meaningful parts which are stored away into a system, ready for retrieval at a later date. This verification word study is so rapid that many good spellers do not even know that they have performed the analysis and storage. It is towards this automatic process that we are directing the children. If they possess a good coding system and good writing habits, such as efficient handwriting and checking, they are most likely to achieve this automatic process.

Dictionary Work

Most children have by now at least been introduced to the dictionary and now they should complete all the activities described in Chapter Seven so that they become adept at using this essential resource.

Many teachers will feel that this proposed spelling curriculum does not give the children enough words to learn. However, it should be stressed that this curriculum shows the children how to learn to spell, which is a far more complicated process than merely teaching them how to spell words. Once a child knows how to learn to spell then this becomes a continuous process which will be useful throughout his life.

Spelling and Writing

Finally, the teacher must remember the purpose of spelling and that is to communicate in writing. If the teacher omits the opportunity for writing in her spelling curriculum then she has wasted not only her time but the children's as well. Her aim must be to encourage the children to become *active, confident writers.*

One of the ingredients of spelling is to write from *memory* but unfortunately this factor is often overlooked by teachers. Children in the classroom often spend a considerable amount of time completing exercises which require them to select the correct word from a list and insert it in a given sentence. If this is attempting to teach them to spell then it is unlikely to succeed. It is teaching them to copy correctly, but this is not spelling.

Copying is important in the early stages of learning to spell and it is required in the familiarisation of letters and new words. But once the learner is able to work from memory, this must be used instead, and the prop of copying needs to be removed. Once this support is removed a child might feel a little unsure of his ability, but he will gain confidence if the teacher praises his efforts.

Remember that copying is practised many, many times until the learner feels he knows the letter or word. Allowing the child to copy it once only would be insufficient for most learners, yet this is what is done in many exercises. The child merely copies the word into the ready-made sentence and unless he already knows the word or is a good speller it is unlikely that this word will be retained in his memory. Often the child is not even allowed to compose his own sentence, so a valuable opportunity to write has been lost and the child takes on the role of a passive copyist.

If we are to encourage the child to be an active, confident writer we must be honest in our tasks and realistic in the writing opportunities we provide. A child's writing, especially in the initial stages, is often simply constructed and rather untidy, but through his own efforts he will gradually acquire his own style. Given encouragement it is likely that his own sentences will far surpass the rather bland exercises found in many textbooks and work cards. As soon as the child has mastered some of the basic words let him write his own message – on scrap paper if you wish – and allow him the opportunity to know what it feels like to communicate on paper. Two lines of real communication are better than twenty pages of exercises.

To begin with the tasks will be very simple, such as writing his name on a Christmas or birthday card. As he improves he will want to add the person's name and perhaps a message. Two examples are given which the teacher might like to photocopy. These can be folded and used to augment the lovely cards which the children often make in their art work.

Children often like to write message to their friends; perhaps telling them news which they did not have time to tell the class in the usual news time. Once a week have a post box where the children can 'mail' their messages. This will provide opportunity for their reading as well as their writing. Let them write their own letters, and unless they are able to write formally styled letters do not make this into 'letter-writing' practice; that would spoil the fun. Some children may become over-excited and be rather silly at first but if it becomes a regular event they will soon settle down. One word of warning, though – make sure that everyone receives a letter, even if you have to write some yourself!

It is often through letters that children become aware of the power and pleasure of writing. Letters are one of the main sources of writing for adults and so it is as well to spend quite some time on these activities. Pages of decorative notepaper, suitable for boys, are included here for photocopying. These could be used for 'special' letters which the child wishes to write. These letters should still be simply constructed with 'to' and 'from' instead of the usual salutations. Try to restrict the child's writing as little as possible.

Always try to foster the desire to write. Do not ask for too much but always praise good quality. Too often we ask the child to 'write a page' although he may not have a page-worth of writing to give and the result is a page of padding. Encourage the child to write his own thoughts in his own style and perhaps even his own spelling, and then at least you have something to work on together.

Photocopy masters are provided on pages 87–89.

Examples of decorative notepaper

_____ _____

_____ _____

_____ _____

_____ _____

_____ _____

_____ _____

_____ _____

_____ _____

_____ _____

PART THREE
OTHER RELATED AREAS

9 Remedial Teaching

Introduction

The poor speller is not some sort of biological quirk of Nature, although such assumptions are still made about children who are failing in this subject. They are labelled as being 'auditory weak' or 'visually weak' and we have 'clinics' where 'diagnoses' are made. The use of such terminology carries the suggestion that there is something wrong with the child and some sort of corrective treatment is necessary. However, how good is the teaching of spelling in schools? Are some children failing to make satisfactory progress because of poor or non-existent teaching? It is far easier to blame the child than the school.

Schonell in 1942 described the causes of disability in spelling as:
1. weak visual ability
2. weak auditory ability
3. both
4. feeling of inferiority
5. speech defects and faulty pronunciation
6. carelessness.

There was no mention of inadequate teaching. Nor is it made clear by Schonell whether these are causes or symptoms of spelling difficulty.

To explain this point let us consider an adult in a learning situation. Imagine someone who is learning to drive. Because he is learning, he is unsure of himself and displays nervousness, even though he might be making good progress. If he subsequently fails his driving test, do we say the nervousness was the cause of his poor performance or just a characteristic found among learner drivers? Obviously it could be either, but it should be remembered that nervous drivers do pass their tests, and the best way of removing some of the nervousness is to make them more skilled at handling a car.

When people learn to drive they bring to the task quite different backgrounds, personalities and learning strategies. Some learn easily, and others take considerable time mastering the skill, but clinics are not set up to diagnose the learner's traits! The instructors analyse the skill and therefore see which aspects need further practice, and since spelling is a skill teachers should employ similar techniques. Rather than looking at the poor speller to discover what might be inhibiting his learning, we should be looking at the teaching to see whether we are teaching all the necessary skills.

Considering Schonell's six 'causes' of disability in spelling, is it surprising to find that the poor speller has a feeling of inferiority? It is true that many poor spellers do exhibit these feelings but they are generally confined to spelling. As soon as the learner learns to spell his feeling of inferiority disappears, just as when the learner driver passes his test he gains in confidence as he drives more.

This chapter will not, therefore, diagnose the poor speller in an attempt to find the cause of spelling difficulties, but will instead suggest ways to encourage the remedial child to make a fresh start. Although the BBC booklet gives this warning to teachers: 'Good spellers, on the whole, are born rather than made, so you need to be realistic about your ambitions . . .' (BBC Adult Literacy Handbook p. 41), such contentions are refuted here. There is no evidence to suggest that 'good spellers are born rather than made'. Some children find spelling easier than others, but given good teaching there is no reason why the majority of children should not achieve a functional spelling competence. We will now consider the important part played by the teacher in the remedial situation.

Remedial teaching is not just good first teaching; it requires far more than that. The remedial teacher has to be knowledgeable about her subject, but also has to have flair and empathy with her students. She cannot simply go over the work they should have covered in earlier years, for whilst they require this knowledge, the activities described in the First Stage are too young for these older students.

The other factor which is probably of prime importance, and marks the difference between first teaching and remedial work, is the fact that these children know they have failed. They camouflage their failure in various ways from bravado to tears, from dogged persistence in following strategies which nevertheless do not work, to the butterfly mind which tries nothing. However, the majority do want to learn but a fresh approach must be used, in which they do not fail, and which does not seem childish.

Typewriters

Personally I have found the typewriter a most useful piece of equipment for teaching spelling to the remedial student. First, it is not considered a remedial apparatus and in fact it has high kudos among the learner's classmates. Second, the print is clear and looks professional, especially to a child whose own handwriting may be particularly poor. Third, the machine operates quickly and in the correct left to right direction. This final point overcomes slowness and confusion over direction.

The most suitable typewriters are simple, manual portables which can be stored easily and set up by the children themselves. There is no evidence to suggest that remedial children require special, large print or a keyboard which is in lower case, or particular non-confusing letters such as 'ɑ' for 'a' and 'ɡ' for 'g'. Most children are aware of the various styles of print found in their everyday lives.

Unfortunately, many machines are wasted in schools because the teachers have been unaware of their advantages and disadvantages. First, let us consider two opposing views. Hildreth (1955) says: ' . . . below age seven, the children tend merely to fiddle with the machines. Above that age . . . they can learn typing easily'. (*Teaching Spelling* p. 96–7)

I have used typewriters with children below the age of seven; in fact some of the children were only three years of age, and perhaps their movements might be thought of as 'fiddling', but on the other hand they seemed to be exploring the machines. It depends what you expect from young children. If they spend some minutes watching the keys hitting the paper, or the ribbon crawling along as they type, or try all the keys in turn, is this bad? Even a very young child learns something from a typewriter if he is allowed to use it at his own level.

The other contentious view in the Hildreth quotation assumes that children will 'catch' typing. Some teachers assume that not only will the children have no difficulty typing out their work but they will also be able to compose straight on to the typewriter.

Typing is a skill which is not easily mastered, particularly without proper teaching. Not only does the operator have to press the right keys, but he has to remember to use the space bar, the shift key for capital letters and to insert correct punctuation marks which sometimes also requires use of the shift key. A child would find it very difficult to make a fair copy of his written notes, and unless the work is very short he is likely to become frustrated by his failure to complete the task correctly.

And requiring the child to compose his work straight on to the typewriter is, of course, even more difficult than that mentioned above. Even an experienced typist finds it difficult to compose straight on to the machine.

Both the above tasks do not seem to have clear objectives concerning why typewriters should be used. If it is only to make a clear copy then the child should be encouraged to write neatly, making the finished work as attractive and individual as possible with coloured pens for underlining and so on. He is likely to have more sense of pride in his finished article than a piece of poorly typed work.

However, typewriters can be used with considerable advantage when the tasks are more simple, at least in the initial stages.

First the child has to be familiar with all the letter shapes as described in the First Stage, Chapter Five. Ideally, the letters should be written in order for the child to become thoroughly familiar with each letter shape, but by now the older child is bored with such activities. However, the typewriter can rekindle an interest in letters. This can be introduced as a task which helps him locate all the letters on the keyboard quickly and without hesitation. Let the child explore the keyboard using any finger he wishes, for we are not teaching him to type, but rather using the typewriter to teach spelling.

Next, when the child thinks he knows the position of each letter, he can be told a letter which he has to find as quickly as possible, then on to another letter and so on. These letters can be given by the teacher especially if she wishes to use this activity as a test to ascertain which letters the child does not know or is confused about. However, if there are two children working with typewriters they can give each other letters to find and this can lighten the teacher's task in the early stages. As the keyboard is in capital letters and the keys in lower case, the children learn the connection without any formal teaching.

This hunt-the-key activity has not, of course, taught them to write the letter from memory but they can at least recognise the correct capital letter. The writer has found ten year olds who still are uncertain about letters. Not only do they confuse the old chestnut 'b' and 'd', but also confuse 'v' and 'n' for 'u', and 'w' for 'm'. Therefore the teacher will need to devise activities which enable the child to write all letters neatly and accurately. The sort of activities will depend very much upon the child's age and temperament, but whatever it is, the task needs to be repeated many times to build up certainty about all letters.

94

Writing

For the slightly older child, handwriting practice might afford an opportunity to become familiar with writing each letter. To make it more interesting, the child could use coloured pens and be encouraged to assess his best letter on each line which he could indicate with a little tick. Above all he should feel a sense of enjoyment and achievement about his writing, for in many ways it is an artistic expression of himself. Some particularly artistic teachers are able to develop this writing practice into an art lesson where the child devises letter styles appropriate to word meanings, such as 'slim' in long slender lettering or 'strong' in squarish, squat letters, and this idea can be developed into labels for pop groups, and so on. Lettering is therefore seen as creative and fun, not something boring which is executed in a standard form to the teacher's direction.

Sometimes this lifting of restrictions and encouragement of personal expression can result in an offering in glorious technicolour. However, most children soon settle down to write in one particular colour and, after all, the teacher has achieved her objective, which was to get the children to put pen to paper.

Common Words

Again the typewriter can be used to stimulate involvement in what could, otherwise, be a rather boring activity. The child is shown a card containing the first common words and is told that, since these words are used so frequently, it would be useful if he learnt to type them quickly and easily. It is most likely he already knows how to spell all these words so he will be able to concentrate upon the typing skill. Again he can use any finger he wishes, although it is better if he now uses his thumb for the space bar, as this aids typing.

He can start with any word he likes, and the task is to type the word for as often as he wishes, so that finally he can type it quickly without looking at the master copy on the card. When he thinks he is able to do that, he ticks the word and selects another, and so on. He will encounter the word 'I' which requires a capital letter, and so will be introduced to the shift key in a meaningful way.

When he has completed all the words, he can write out little sentences or phrases containing as many of these words as possible. These should not be given by the teacher but, as mentioned earlier, should be composed by the child himself, in his group if necessary.

Obviously other words will have to be introduced, so it is wise for the teacher to check the sentences before the child proceeds with the typing. The sentence is written by the child on a slip of paper and presented to the teacher for checking. (By now there should be no mistakes among the common words the child has been typing.) Once the sentence is checked the child returns to the typewriter and sees how often he can type the sentence without errors. The following day, if the child says he knows the sentence, the teacher can dictate the whole sentence and the child can either type or write it. Do not be too harsh if he gets some of it wrong, but instead try to encourage the parts which are right. If he still needs practice using these words ask him for different sentences and continue until he is absolutely sure of these basic words.

The learning of these common words has been built up slowly, it is active, the feedback is immediate, the child works at his own pace and he is able to achieve success. Obviously, typing errors will be made but they will not ruin the whole work for the child is only practising, not typing a finished piece of work.

It is suggested that each typing session lasts approximately twenty minutes, which ensures that children do not become too fatigued resulting in a pile-up of errors. They remain motivated for the next session and the typewriter is freed for use by another child.

As the child becomes more proficient in typing, more of the common words are introduced, but alongside this the child can be given activities which teach him to become familiar with some of the basic coding patterns.

Coding Skills

Often children ask why the typewriter is not constructed alphabetically. There are many reasons for this but one the writer usually offers is that certain letters are used a lot so they are positioned in an accessible place, and letters which often appear together are placed so that they can be typed easily. Often this results in a discussion upon whether they agree or disagree with this proposition.

The child selects a letter pair, such as 'er' or 'th' and writes out a few words containing the pair, which are checked for correct spelling by the teacher. He then types these words to see whether he considers the keyboard positioning helps or hinders. For the next typing session, he can bring some more words containing the letter pair, so affording further practice. Obviously he cannot type out all words containing the 'er' or 'th' pair but it is making him aware of familiar patterns.

From then on he can select a weekly letter group with help from the teacher, and produce words for typing as described above. Not only will this help his typing but it will start him off on the 'group hunts' described in Chapter Six.

The typewriter is particularly effective when a child is considering letter patterns such as 'same-change-same' in words like *piece*, or doubling in words like *putting*, for the learner soon discovers that typing these patterns is rapid and rhythmic.

When the remedial child first encounters coding skills he seldom finds a great number of words containing each letter group, but gradually, especially working as a group, the number of words increases until he is able to take part in 'group hunts' as described in earlier chapters.

The familiarisation stage is therefore carried out largely through the use of the typewriter. As before, allow the children plenty of time to become familiar with all the letters and the most common letter groups.

Typing sentences

Through work in the common word section, the child will gradually be able to tackle the typing of small sentences. It is suggested that his first real typing should be simple instructions, such as 'Please turn off the lights' or 'Have you closed the hamster cage?' Such sentences involve a fair amount of work but the child can have many attempts at the sentence and then select the best one for use in the classroom.

He may also wish to type out a simple label for his own work, such as a map title, or name and subject for his work books, or he may wish to type out his address for his school bag. The main aim in these activities is to get him using writing for a purpose, even if the purpose is little more than a labelling task.

It is likely that the child will find the above work can be completed more effectively by neat printing, especially if he has been receiving handwriting practice and so now feels that his writing is able to stand up to scrutiny. Gradually, as his writing improves interest in the typewriter will wane and this is good, for if he wishes to learn to type properly he should receive correct instruction in touch typing. The typewriter has been used here to get the child returning to written communication, this process being made more interesting and easier by use of the machine.

Three examples of pages from a typing booklet follow, two are suitable for photocopying.

Name: _____

Name: _____

Example of a page from a typing booklet

```
Type the word until you can do it
without looking at the word in this
book.
Tick the box, then go on to the
next word.


lowest    [    ]        stayed    [    ]

remain    [    ]        damage    [    ]

worry     [    ]        else      [    ]

brought   [    ]        through   [    ]

mistake   [    ]        entered   [    ]
```

Other Activities

The teacher is advised to consult the chapters in Part Two for other activities which can be used in teaching spelling to the remedial student. It is the first stage, Chapter Five, which is the most difficult to put across to the remedial child for he does not want to write, and feels he cannot do so. Once he has been shown that it can be enjoyable, then he is able to take full advantage of the activities devised for the average learner. The child should soon be able to embark upon the activities described in Chapters Six and Seven.

Such activities might include word bingo for common words, and the dictionary games. Once the child realises he is able to spell most of the ordinary words he will then be free to concentrate upon the more troublesome ones. If he is also skilled in consulting a diction-ary to check these troublesome words for himself, then much of his problem disappears. Armed with this basic knowledge, he will be able to put pen to paper without feeling the task is beyond him, for now he has control over at least the groundwork of the task.

More than anything else the teacher must instil confidence in the remedial child, trying to show him that he does in fact know some words rather than making him aware of how many words he cannot spell. The words known to him should be useful words which he desires to use in his writing, even if it is only accolades to his favourite football team or pop group. Writing must have a purpose and it should be an expressive means of communiction. The skilled remedial teacher knows how to utilise the child's interests as a means of sustaining educational progress. This is as true of spelling as of any other subject.

If a slow learner still finds writing difficult or unpleasant, an activity such as Trackwords might help to stimulate an interest in words.

Trackwords

Trackwords are often useful to stimulate an interest in words. Even a child who is reluctant to write anything may work quite happily with a friend when trying to unscramble a trackword grid.

The task is to try and find as many words as possible tracking from square to adjacent square in any direction. The same square cannot be used twice in the same word. All words are counted, including proper nouns, and it is often wise to allow abbreviations as this can extend their vocabulary.

The same trackword grid can be used for younger or older pupils, since each person will find words they know. The young child will succeed by finding say, three words, and the older child will suc-ceed by finding thirty words. The child should not have any sense of failure when working on a trackword. Do not make it into a competition but rather an activity which allows for individual dis-coveries.

Blank grids have been provided for photocopying so that the teacher can provide a variety of trackwords for her pupils.

Examples of complete trackword grids and blank grids

b	o	a
l	e	t
f	h	s

p	n	e	g	u
l	a	e	s	c
i	m	t	h	x
k	y	a	b	o
e	r	i	f	w

10 Testing Spelling

Most schools test spelling at some time or other, and in many schools the ritual weekly test is common practice. As so much time is devoted to the testing of spelling this chapter considers just this activity.

First let us consider the achievement test of spelling, the aim of which is to compare the child's performance with other children of the same age. Normative tests are widely used in education, but with regard to spelling, these tests have to be treated with caution.

Such tests usually consist of lists of harder and harder words and it is assumed that the older children can spell the more difficult words and the younger children will be able to spell only the easier words. Hence, achievement tests are sometimes recorded in years and months but such test results make assumptions about the words which do not necessarily relate to the child's spelling ability.

For example what is meant by more difficult words? Do we really know which words are difficult for each age group, for it is upon this basis that the tests stand or fall? It is easy to think of longer words as being more difficult, but this is not necessarily correct. A long word such as *destination* is easier than the word *aeon* for many reasons. It is probably more familiar to the child, and it has a closer sound/letter correspondence. Even the spelling pattern 'tion' which can be considered a hard spot is a common feature of many words.

If we equate difficult with unusual or complex spelling patterns this might seem more profitable. Under these conditions the words chosen for the test would cover spelling patterns of increasing complexity.

However, this still does not solve the problem of which words should be included in tests, for usage plays an important part in the spelling process. If a child is particularly interested in air travel, he might well be familiar with words such as *aeroplane* and *astronaut* but he might experience difficulty with words such as *join* and *calm*. His spelling vocabulary is influenced by his requirements, not governed by the complexities of the spelling patterns of the words involved. Generally a word in common use is going to be spelt correctly. This means that if the achievement test contains unusual words, but nevertheless easy spelling patterns, then there is the probability that scores will be low.

We must also consider what is meant by a high score on an achievement test. Does it mean the child will be able to spell all other similar words correctly? If he spells *ear* correctly does it mean he will also be able to spell *pear*, *heart*, and *search*? Usually if the child spells *ear* correctly it means that he has merely spelt that word right on that particular occasion, and we cannot generalise about his probable performance on other words, even if they contain the same letter pattern.

These comments raise the problem of attaching to the pupil a spelling competence from just one sample of words. We cannot grade children according to their spelling achievement in years and months for it is not yet known, with any degree of certainty, which words children can and cannot spell at different ages, nor do we know whether the ability to spell some words indicates a general spelling ability.

Vincent and Crosswell (1976) said of spelling tests:
'Only a few standardised tests of spelling are available. Schonell's *Graded Word Spelling Test* and sub-tests II of the *Standard Reading Tests* are the most widely used and both have norms which are probably now out of date . . . There has been little research into the validity of any of the ways these tests measure spelling achievement.' (*Reading Tests in the Classroom* p. 96)

Vernon (1963) had previously questioned the validity of spelling tests when he said:
'Spelling tests sample the child's spelling . . . While this is quite legitimate, the trouble is that testers are continually tempted to infer beyond the behaviour itself – to regard the spelling test as measuring spelling ability in general!' (*Personality Assessment: A Critical Survey* p. 213)

My own investigations show that poor spellers vary their attempts at the same word from one occasion to another. Not only do the errors vary, but on some occasions the word is spelt correctly, and then is misspelt in a bizarre way on subsequent occasions. This instability is more common among the very poorest spellers. So it seems that any spelling test given to very poor spellers is going to be somewhat unreliable. If a teacher assesses a child's spelling ability upon just one test on one occasion, then the teacher is likely to be misinformed.

However, many teachers use actual spelling achievements tests only very occasionally, although the normal weekly test is a ritual in many schools, and this type of test will now be considered.

Weekly Spelling Tests

One of the first questions to ask is, 'Why do we give weekly spelling tests?' The answers to this will vary but the question must be answered honestly by the teacher, for the way we administer the test will be influenced by what we are trying to achieve.

If we are merely trying to assess general spelling achievement then there is no need to test weekly. A battery of tests given once a term or even yearly is all that is required, provided that the results are treated with caution as mentioned above.

If we are attempting to measure the child's spelling improvement then this is personal and does not need to be compared with other children in the class, or to be normative in any way. Spot testing using the child's free writing is possibly the most efficient way of dealing with this for it will indicate not only the type of words the child is trying to use, but also the number of words written within a given time. A subjective measure is all that is required for most teaching purposes when one is considering a child's progress. The mark itself is of very little importance, but the papers should be kept so that comparisons can be made at the end of the year. The trained eye of the teacher will easily be able to spot whether the child has truly improved in vocabulary, presentation and style. The teacher is not concerned whether Johnnie can spell *disestablishmentarian*, but rather whether he can spell, or give a good rendering, of the words he needs to use.

The other reason commonly given in defence of weekly tests is that the teacher is trying to get the child to learn at least ten words per week. Excellent. But what actually happens in practice?

At the beginning of the week, usually on Monday morning, the children are all given ten words to be learnt by the end of the week. The teacher normally writes the words on the blackboard, sometimes giving their meanings and emphasising the tricky parts by underlining or drawing lines where the words should be divided into syllables. The children copy these ten words into their books.

No further work is done in school upon the words. The teacher considers her job to be finished with regard to the spellings, and the children are supposed to take the list of words home to learn on their own or ask for help from their parents. On reflection, isn't this a rather strange way of teaching anything? Suppose this practice was followed in Mathematics. The teacher would give the children ten equations and tell them to take them home and be ready for testing on Friday. No doubt the parents would complain that it was the teacher's job to teach but, as far as is known, not a murmur is heard when the subject is spelling. The practice of taking words home to learn has been going on for so long that it is now accepted without question. Of course, there is nothing wrong with it provided some teaching has taken place at school, and provided the child has knowledge of some methods which will help him to learn the words.

Many parents test the child on the words, so the child receives a pre-test before the Friday test, but this is not necessarily *teaching spelling*, although it might help the child to gain a higher mark. Also, testing is often squeezed in between household chores and so the parent simply asks the word and the child recites the correct letters. Such reciting is adequate for good spellers who can reel off the letters at a tremendous pace, but for the child who experiences any difficulty it is important that he be given the opportunity to write down the spelling, and to keep on having another go at it until he feels it looks right – or is as near as he can get.

Returning to the school situation, what happens when Friday arrives and the child receives his spelling test? The following description is based upon classroom observations of many competent teachers.

The children number down one to ten in their books, then the teacher calls out the words, usually in isolation. She does not place the word within the context of a sentence. When all ten words have been called out the children change books with their neighbours and the teacher reads out the correct spelling. The ticks are added up, the score written in the book and it is then handed back to the owner. The teacher then, often with record book in hand, asks each child to call out his score which is duly noted and poor scorers, especially boys, are reprimanded.

As these weekly tests are given in order to teach spelling, one wonders how educational the activity is in practice. Does it teach spelling? Does it create a positive attitude towards spelling? Does a child's spelling improve as a result of these tests?

Answering the last question first, yes, it does seem as if testing a child on the same word often results in a higher score on the second occasion. Of course, this does not necessarily mean the teacher has actually taught the child to spell, or that the child's spelling has improved. It just means that the child is getting better at doing that particular test. However, since the teacher displayed an interest in spelling, there is more likelihood that her pupils will also concern themselves with spelling, and since they are required to take part in a spelling test each week there is more of a chance their spelling will improve. Therefore, if in doubt about whether to test or not, I would definitely say 'test', although the teacher should seek to make the test as educational as possible. The following suggests minor amendments which are easily incorporated into a weekly spelling test and result in a greatly improved activity.

Consider the words to be used in the test – where do they come from? Sometimes they are taken from a published word list and the difficulty here is that often they are outside the child's range of interests. Usually, they are selected because they contain a spelling pattern, such as 'ie' in *chief, view, siege, field* and *sieve*. On other occasions teachers give words which have been found difficult by many pupils in their free writing, or words connected with current projects or subject requirements. The latter methods of word selection are best since they use words which the children are likely to require, and therefore there is some purpose in learning them.

Although drawing a child's attention to spelling patterns is more likely to result in a general spelling improvement, there seems little point in the teacher presenting the children with the spelling patterns and words all neatly tied up, with nothing for the children to do except learn somebody else's list. Why not give the children a choice of spelling patterns? The whole class can vote for the pattern of the week, or different groups can select their own pattern. This would at least make them feel involved in the task.

The children can find a number of words containing this spelling pattern from which they select their own words for testing. The better spellers can select more words than the poorer spellers, or more difficult words, but the practice of giving all the children the same words seems odd, and runs contrary to the view held nowadays that children should be taught according to their own levels and requirements. I have seen excellent teachers using individual work cards as well as carefully organised group work, but who still give out ten words to all the children, as if somehow spelling lay outside the theory of individual learning patterns. No doubt they have just not considered the implications of their actions with regard to spelling, for if questioned I am sure they would wish to teach spelling at least at group work level.

Returning to the idea of the children selecting their own words, the immediate outcry from some teachers would be that the children would select only the easy words, but in my own experience this is seldom the case. In fact with the remedial child, at least, the problem is often one of drawing attention to the simpler words which they tend to overlook in their desire to spell 'big words'. Even with words based on project work I allow the children to select words they think will be useful for their writing. This is often highly illuminating for the teacher. One group of nine year old slow learners gave the following words, based upon a field study trip in the Yorkshire Dales:

> waterfall
> cave
> sedimentary
> igneous
> metamorphic
> youth (they stayed at a youth hostel)
> Mr Campbell (their class teacher)
> Ingleton

They chose only eight spellings for a child seldom considers the number of words significant and will choose just the number of words he thinks he needs and can cope with. If the words are particularly difficult, let the children choose fewer words, or more if they feel they can cope with a large number.

In the above example the words were highly relevant to their requirements. I would not have given them the geological words, thinking them too difficult, but in this I was proved wrong and they delighted in their mastery of 'big words'. Nor would I have selected the last three in the list. Firstly, I would not have realised the need for the word *youth*, nor realised the need for proper nouns in the spelling list, especially the teacher's name. However, proper nouns constantly present stumbling blocks even to adults and the children's inclusion of them in the spelling list made me appreciate how seldom we bother to teach such words.

Thus we have finally arrived at a selection of words suitable for testing. The teacher can vary the approach, maybe using spelling patterns for two weeks, then a week on project words followed by a week testing common words. It will be appreciated that the selection of words by the children is an educational task in itself; for the children have done the work and not the teacher, and really this is the way the children like it. It might take slightly longer but instead of the teacher presenting the children with a list of words which are often of little interest to them, the children have to present the teacher with a list of words they themselves have chosen. The learning process is already nearly complete, for the children have been involved.

The way the children will set about learning the words has already been described in Chapters Six and Seven. Again the children should be largely responsible for selecting the method they consider appropriate for each word, as not all words require the same treatment, nor does each child respond identically to one method.

Leaving aside the learning process, let us now consider the Friday test and see how this can be improved upon with very little effort on the teacher's part.

The first stage need not be altered. The children write down the required number and the teacher calls out the word. (However it is usually best for the word to be given in a sentence as well, to make certain the child knows exactly which word is required.)

The next stage is normally that of exchanging papers, but why do we do this? To stop any cheating? But does 'cheating' have any meaning in an educational activity? The child is merely correcting his own work. If we are concerned with obtaining a score for our record books then the *teacher* should mark all the papers. Exchanging papers is a half-hearted attempt which neither achieves a totally reliable score (since a child seldom likes putting crosses against his friend's work), nor is it an educational activity. In fact the only thing it does achieve with any certainty is the embarrassment of the poor speller when his friends not only see how bad his attempts are, but are licenced to correct his work. Allowing children to mark each other's test papers is a harmful activity, for the class is a social group with all the loyalties, fears, hate and awe that go with all such groups. A teacher who is good at spelling herself might underrate these effects, but as a poor speller myself I well remember as a child suffering agonies wondering who would be given my paper to mark. On a more humorous note, my own son told me once that he didn't have to learn any spellings because he sat next to his friend!

So if the teacher requires reliable scores let her mark the papers herself, but if the weekly tests are to help children with their spellings, let them mark their own and do not collect the scores; the scores are unimportant. If you feel there must be some inquest afterwards, simply ask them which words they thought were the most difficult and why, or how many children felt they performed better this week. Show that you are interested in their performance, not just in their scores.

Scoring

Scoring is seldom given much thought, for it is common practice to accord one mark for correct spelling and zero mark for any error. However, as it seems spelling gradually improves for each word, a marking system which acknowledges a good attempt is most likely to encourage the child to continue improving. By providing inter-mediate steps, the teacher can encourage the very poor speller to try and get some of it right. For example, she could award two marks for correct spelling and one mark for only a minor error.

The present system of awarding one mark or nothing does not seem good educational practice. The spelling task is very difficult for some children, and therefore at the outset they know they are unlikely to gain anything. This must increase their expectation of failure. By awarding an intermediate mark it also means that the child must mark his own work carefully; studying the errors to see whether he could qualify for a mark. Scrutiny of errors on the child's part is a necessary step if he is ever to make improvements, for he is forced to compare the closeness of his attempt with the correct spelling. He is less likely merely to put a cross and move on to the next word. In other words, his attitude towards misspellings becomes more constructively critical.

Needless to say, the answers cannot now be given out orally as the children need time to compare their spelling attempt with the cor-rect form. The teacher can write the word upon the blackboard, but even better is to ask for volunteers from the class to do the writing upon the board. Children usually love writing on the blackboard and it would be a very unusual class indeed which did not provide many volunteers for each word. If the teacher finds that this type of marking is taking up too much time, then three or four volunteers can be writing at the board at the same time.

This description of the weekly spelling test has been considered as a large group activity. If the testing is to be carried out in small groups or even individually in some case, then it is suggested that a tape recorder be used, or the testing spread over a few days. The child himself can say the words on to the tape recorder, but he must remember to allow sufficient time between words for him either to be able to write down his answers, or for the machine to be switched off without losing part of the next word. (With some children the teacher needs to check the recording too, either because it might be too indistinct or because the children have recorded the spelling as well!)

Sentence Test

A slightly different type of test which has proved useful with very poor spellers is the sentence test. The word is given, but the child has to write a short sentence containing the word in its exact form, i.e. no plurals or past tenses etc. are allowed. If the child is unable to think of a sentence at that moment he can write the word and return to it at the end of the test. Allow funny or odd sentences provided they make sense – this somehow encourages the boys in particular to write! At the end of the test the children are invited to read out any good sentences they have. It is usually necessary to limit each child to one sentence otherwise the test would take all day to complete. The children give themselves a mark if they think they have managed to place the word in context.

This extra mark for context ensures that no child gets zero marks for the test, and it also seems that very poor spellers perform better on this sentence type of test. The reason is somewhat speculative, but it could be that the child is over-anxious when given a list of words, and that this anxiety is diluted when he has more writing to do. The set words are then marked for spelling, so that each sentence has at least two marks; one for content and one for correct spelling of the set word. It will be noticed that the ordinary spelling test is now flowing over into word usage and this seems the correct direction for it to take. Whilst we have to learn to spell words, we also have to use the words in sentences.

The sentence test naturally leads on to the question of dictation tests. These are difficult, and the underlying principle is quite different. As an adult, one has only to accept dictation from another to appreciate how difficult these tests are. First, the subject matter is often outside the recipient's knowledge or interest. Second, the style is different from our own, for we each have many styles which we use in different contexts. Thus in addition to the spellings, we have also to think about different subject matter and style, which really has little to do with testing spelling. Dictation of children's own phrases or sentences has been considered in Part Two, but in that case it was an activity devised to encourage children to think and write in phrases, and was not used in a testing situation.

110

Pre-testing

Another matter to be considered is the value of pre-testing or testing the children on the same words on different occasions. The more practice the child gets in writing words, the more likely he is to achieve success. By all means, give the children a pre-test at the beginning of the week just to show them which words need learning, and even if they have all the words right one week they can still be given them on another occasion. Words often slip out of the child's memory, especially if they have not been used very often. If they do get all the words correct yet again, what a lovely feeling of success they will feel!

If the aim of the weekly test is educational, then the teacher should discard any idea of the results conforming to the bell-shaped curve. In this case we want them all to succeed with their particular words. Spelling tests should not be dreaded by children. The tests should be tailored to the particular child, not made more and more difficult, as if we were taking part in a high jump contest where everyone experiences failure – even the winner. In spelling the children should all feel they are going to succeed, for nothing succeeds like success.

When a child has become a competent speller, and spelling mistakes are very rare, then the teacher can stop teaching spelling to that child and let him concentrate upon his own writing. There is absolutely no point in plying the child with more and more difficult words which are probably outside his vocabulary anyway. As a parallel, once a child has shown himself proficient at 'tables', we do not progress into the 20s, 30s and 100s times tables. The child has demonstrated that he possesses a working knowledge, and except for occasional checks nothing more needs to be done. In spelling, the child may also need occasional checks as his vocabulary extends but if he is adept at using a dictionary no more teaching is necessary.

At the other extreme if the teacher has a particularly poor speller, then that child will need special monitoring. The following suggests a new scoring scheme which involves the teacher in considerably more work but nevertheless is able to assess a child's performance even when the child has failed to get any words at all spelt correctly.

Analysed Scoring

This scoring scheme can be used for any type of spelling test, for it does not specify which words are to be tested but concentrates upon how they are scored. Using the normal dichotomous marking scheme (one mark for correct spelling and zero for any error) a great deal of information is wasted. When a child makes a mistake we cannot tell how severe the error was, using this method. Was one letter omitted or was the attempt a complete jumble of letters? The analysed scoring scheme scores each word twice, once for correct letters and secondly for correct order.

An example will help to illustrate this. For the word *daughter* the scoring would be:

daughter
1 1 1 1 1 1 1 1 = 8 marks for letters
1 2 2 2 2 2 2 1 = 14 marks for order
= 22 marks for correct spelling

The reason that only one mark is given for the first and last letters under ordering is that research shows that these are usually the letters most easily remembered.

Extra letters are ignored except in the very few cases when full marks would have been obtained for a misspelling. For example, 'daurghter' would have gained 22 marks, and in these cases one mark is subtracted for each extra letter. Thus 'daurghter' would be accorded 21 marks out of the possible 22 marks.

Another amendment to this marking scheme concerns ordering, and again an example will illustrate the problem. When a word such as *daughter* is written as 'daghter' it means that, as the third letter is missing, all other letters are not strictly in their correct place. For instance, 'g' should be in the fourth place but now is in third place and so on. However, it seems unfair to deny the closeness of this attempt and so normal scoring is resumed if subsequently three or more letters are in the correct sequence.

To illustrate how this scoring measures spelling errors the following examples from actual test papers show the way in which the closer the attempt to the correct spelling is, the greater the score:

Word: *daughter*		Word: *headache*		Word: *cough*	
dotr	5	edake	7	cof	5
dorter	10	hedake	9	couf	8
darter	13	headek	12	couth	10
dauter	16	headack	17	*cough	13
daghter	19	headace	19		
daugter	19	headacke	19		
*daughter	22	headach	20		
		*headache	22	*correct spelling	

The aggregate score for a whole test of say twenty words would not provide an easily recognisable score, as in dichotomous marking where 10 out of 20 means ten words have been spelt correctly out of a possible 20 words. Using the analysed scoring scheme the raw score could be say, 211 out of 314, and it is therefore useful to use percentages when comparing a child's performance on subsequent tests.

Using the aggregate score, expressed as a percentage, it was found that those children scoring less than 60 per cent of possible marks had a very poor knowledge of the coding system used in English spelling, and these children could be considered 'at risk'. Of course, it does depend on the difficulty of the words tested. But if a teacher finds that one child persists in misspelling all, or most, words which the rest of the class seem able to spell, then an analysis of his errors using this new scheme might indicate whether his errors were minor ones, perhaps due to carelessness, or whether they indicate a real problem.

If a child scores less than 60 per cent it is suggested that the teacher uses some of the activities outlined in Chapter Six with special reference to the coding system, or Chapter Nine which considers remedial teaching. The teacher will be able to decide which activities are most appropriate for the particular child. He should not consider these 'at risk' pupils as being in any way unusual; the analysed scoring merely shows that their performance indicates that they do not understand the very basic requirements of spelling. It is the teacher's responsibility to clarify the spelling process so that the child is able to make reasonable attempts at words.

The following examples, again from actual test papers, show how errors can be reasonable (based upon a likeness to English) and unreasonable (those which are unlike any English word):

Word	Pupil 1	Pupil 2
lowest	leaset	louest
remain	rain	*remain
worry	*worry	wory
brought	bogaht	brout
mistake	miskte	mestak
stayed	*stayed	*stayed
damage	dagde	*damage
else	*else	*else
through	thgagt	throw
entered	ented	enterd

Word	Pupil 1	Pupil 2
cough	*cough	*cough
spare	*spare	*spare
daughter	dagtaer	daugter
edge	*edge	ege
search	shouh	sutch
nerve	noghn	nuve
health	helegh	helth
direct	diceet	diret
calm	congh	carm
headache	headage	headach
Scores		
Analysed	190	248
Dichotomous	6	6

*correct spelling

It will be noticed that both pupils scored the same mark using the dichotomous scheme, but when the work is analysed, Pupil 2 makes reasonable attempts whereas Pupil 1 not only seems to make wild guesses at words but also seems unsure of letters, e.g. 'congh' for *calm* and 'headage' for *headache*.

However, this analysed scoring scheme does require a considerable amount of time and effort on the part of the teacher. It should therefore be considered useful when monitoring the progress of particular children, but not for use when testing a whole class.

All test results should be treated with caution and common sense by the teacher. One test is of very little use – we all have off days – and even a battery of tests provide only an indication of possible performance. The functional performance of the learner spread over a considerable period of time is a more useful guide to his progress, since it shows whether he is able to communicate competently. This is of course the main aim of learning to spell, whether the learner is five or seventy-five.

11 To the Parent

Introduction

Occasionally one still encounters a school where the parents are considered a hindrance to the child's learning, but luckily such a view is not the norm. After all, the parents have taught the child virtually all he knows before entering school, a formidable task. Also, once a child commences school, the home still provides one of the main sources of learning.

Of course each family provides different kinds of support and learning situations and it is difficult for the school to judge its effect upon the child. For this reason we have some very odd assumptions in the educational world about deprivation, especially among poor families. There is the feeling among educationists that poor families generally provide less experience in literacy, whether it be language, writing or reading, and in order to supplement this loss they establish 'compensatory programmes'.

At the other end of the spectrum, middle class families are sometimes viewed as interfering too much in the child's learning. They show too much concern about their child's progress and worry too much over failures, particularly in literacy, which in this case often means reading and writing. Hence you may find schools hostile or even surprised about any interest you express in your child's performance!

This chapter is not written for either 'type' of parent for, being a parent myself, I consider schools should not try to categorise families. The quality of life within a family is a very personal one and is unlikely to be uncovered by answers to bland statements in questionnaires. Parents are people who care about the welfare of their children – only very rarely are there parents who do not care at all. This chapter is written for the majority of parents who care about their child's spelling skills and wish to help the school make learning as efficient as possible.

Since the help you give is influenced by the child's age and stage of spelling, the following chapter is divided into three parts:
1. the pre-school child
2. supplementing normal teaching
3. helping the remedial child.
Obviously you are unlikely to require all three sections and as some sections contain activities found in other parts of the book, it is recommended that you concentrate only upon the section which most fits your needs.

First, however, please read Chapter Three which gives the background knowledge to the theory behind the activities. You will then be able to assess the progress of your child, and know whether he is understanding spelling rather than just completing tasks. You will hopefully also appreciate just how difficult the task is and so give suitable praise when an obstacle has been overcome. Finally, you may be able to devise different activities which suit your child better than those found in this book.

The Pre-school Child

I have found children able to start learning to spell from the age of two years. Of course, this is only at the familiarisation stage but since this is of prime importance it should not be considered something which can be 'caught' at some later stage. However, a very young child is seldom amenable to being taught anything; he wants to explore on his own and this is to be encouraged in spelling as in anything else. Do not imagine you have to sit the child down and give him a spelling lesson every day or every week. A parent of a two year old child knows how foolish such a suggestion is, for at that age, and for a good deal longer, the child does all its learning 'on the trot'. He seldom sits down for more than one minute. He may not seem to be concentrating, yet is learning constantly. Under such conditions one has to dispel any idea of a set lesson, and instead be ready to utilise any opportunity to learn. This is why the parent must have clear objectives when attempting to teach a young child.

The first objective is to encourage the child to learn one letter which is meaningful to him. This is usually his name, so start by drawing a bold, bright letter and tell him, 'That is N for Neil', He will probably not show any interest or be at all impressed, but this is quite normal and does not mean he is not ready to start learning. Put the 'N' label on his bedroom door or coat peg, but do not sprinkle them everywhere in your first flush of enthusiasm. Try to be casual about the whole matter, for many children do not wish to have something thrust upon them. This is particularly true of the two or three year old who wishes to display his independence.

If by any chance he should want to make his own letter let him try, perhaps using a coloured pen writing over your pencil letter. It will probably be very wobbly, will not very often cover your pencil line and instead of stopping at the end the child may trail the pen all over the paper. Whatever happens do not tell him how to write it or reprimand his effort. He will probably make one attempt and then wander off, but young children quickly tire of any task so do not try to persevere or you will kill any interest he might have.

Next, drop the whole matter for about a week or two unless he expresses any particular wish to write his letter. However, in the meantime be on the lookout for any occasion which gives you a chance to use his name. For example, if he has some sweets, and his brothers or sisters also have some, write their names on the packets to distinguish between them. It is surprising how that prompts them to learn their own initial letter!

Then after a suitable lapse of time write his letter again and see if he knows what it is. The answers can be rather amusing such as 'It's me!' but a parent soon learns to recognise what her offspring means and such an answer shows good knowledge of the letter. You can then let him write over your pencil shape as before, but again do not make the shape too small, and make it boldly. On the other hand, you might find using the blackboard more fun for him and in this instance he could brighten up your white line with coloured chalks.

It is unlikely he will be able to copy the letter shape but if he can, all well and good. At first he may like to make the shape in plasticine or left-over pastry, or perhaps write his shape on misty window panes. At home there are many more interesting ways you can make these shapes, so try to invent your own games. The parent has an advantage over the teacher in having to hand so many resources and only a few children in comparison with the school, and this letter-making stage can be fun. Remember the child will learn only those things which he finds enjoyable, so more than anything else make this early writing fun.

The next stage is to find an opportunity for him to use his letter in a real situation. Signing birthday cards or Christmas cards or gift tags to members of the family is one way. If the child is able to see you doing the same thing then he knows he is taking part in a real task, and if he is able to see other people reading his 'name' then he starts to understand the reasons for writing. This later point is very important, and is almost impossible to convey to a child in the artificial world of the school. The parent is in the real world and can make use of any situation which presents itself, so that the child becomes aware of why people write. For example, the child can watch the parent making out a shopping list, but please remember to print otherwise the child will not have an opportunity to recognise the letter shapes.

Returning to 'his' letter he can also sort out his own Christmas presents by reading his letter, or he can find his letter on his birthday cards. Party invitations also provide another opportunity for children either to write their letter or read their name on an incoming invitation. If the parent is aware of the need to give the child real situations for him either to read or write his letter then it is surprising how often occasions occur. But don't labour the point.

When teaching a pre-school child you have two great advantages on your side. You have plenty of time. Months and months can elapse between his first contact with a letter and subsequent uses of this letter. And it does not matter how many letters he learns. This leads on to the second point; even if the child does not learn any letters he can still learn why people write. It is not just scribble on a piece of paper but a message of some kind, and this latter point is most easily learnt at home.

We will now presume that the child is about three years old and perhaps can write his own letter from memory. If you think the child is ready for another letter, by all means introduce another meaningful one. It could be the initial letter of another member of the family but, if possible, choose one which is easily distinguished from his own. These new letters do not have to be learnt as thoroughly as his own one, at this stage they are merely affording him practice in becoming familiar with different letters so that his hand becomes more controlled. If you possess a blackboard you can pin letter cards nearby so that he can copy any he wishes. At this stage I would hesitate from introducing him to all the alphabet; just choose those letters which have some meaning for him. Also if you think he might soon be ready for it, you can display his name card near the blackboard. If it is a complete name I would advocate using the capital letter for the initial letter but lower case for the rest.

As before, we are trying to get the child to enjoy writing and any medium should be employed. Pastry and plasticine have already been mentioned, but a child might enjoy making big shapes. Give him an old paint brush and some water and let him loose on the

118

garden path or fence or shed. If on holiday at the seaside, try to get him making letters in seaweed, shells or pebbles, or with his foot or spade he can make large letters in the wet sand. Try to be as imaginative as possible, but make sure it is fun for the child. If it isn't fun – leave it alone.

About his third birthday, or later if necessary, give him some writing materials of his own, and something to keep it all in. A plastic seed tray is quite good since it is big enough for paper and pens and light enough for a young child to carry around with him. Give him a large wad of cheap paper and one or two small notebooks of interesting shapes and colours, such as a slimline memo pad, and a little attractive square spiral notebook. Buy him some good quality felt-tipped pens which not only last longer but keep their point longer. Also give him some wax crayons (but not if he is in the habit of writing on walls), a new box of coloured chalks and some soft lead pencils. This stationery set is for him to use and you must not worry if he seems to be steaming through it at a rate of knots. The aim is to get him to feel confident in putting pen to paper and to enjoy this feeling.

After about six months or a year you might consider he knows a few letters well enough to be able to identify other words which start with the same sound. For example, he may be able to link N for Neil with N for *nurse, nail* and *knife*. (The last example starts with the N sound and it is only the sound we are considering here.) Take any consonant he knows well and together try to find objects which start with the same sound. The objects can be arranged by the child on a tray, shelf or coffee table and he can make a large letter card as a centrepiece. To make this card even more interesting it could be a collage card as described in Chapter Five. The display can be added to throughout the next few days, but do not leave it lying around for too long, as the child's interest will soon wane. Also, when you have finished with one letter, do not be tempted to start a new table immediately. Make it a special game, not one which is forever present.

When the child is in his fourth year a writing set is a welcome novelty, especially one such as the Mr Men set which contains not only notepaper, but matching envelopes, postcards and a notebook. Stimulated by this, the child often demands whole words, such as *to* and *from* and *Mummy* and *Daddy*. At this age simply write the word on a slip of paper which the child copies from, and if the words are written backwards or in any order do not deflate him by pointing it out. Just try to read the message as best you can and he will be delighted. If, by any stroke of luck, you have another young child next door or any close neighbour who will receive these weird offerings, let the child post their own 'letters' – they love feeling important doing this sort of work.

Other games which require a small amount of writing are playing shops, at the library and at a jumble sale. A child often likes to have notices such as *open, closed, in, out* and *sale* which they can copy and arrange around their stall, desk or whatever it is. The child is not learning how to spell these words, or even read them, but he is acquiring the knowledge that words are made up of different letters and letters are different shapes. Different letters mean different words.

All these activities are encouraging the child to become familiar with writing so that when he enters school he will have a positive atti- tude towards the skill. The building up of this attitude takes a considerable amount of time and skill, and the caring atmosphere of the home is possibly the best place for the child to learn this ground- work.

Besides this all important attitude, what else might the child be able to do? Well, he might be able to write his name, he might be able to recognise some letters and even be able to write some of them from memory. He may be able to recognise similar sounds which was encouraged through the table of objects game, and he will, most probably have considerable control over writing materials whether it be pens, pencils or chalk. This might not seem very much, but it will provide a good basis upon which the teacher can build.

Supplementing Normal Teaching

It is hoped that few parents have to delve into this section for the simple reason that the teaching of spelling at their child's school should be sufficient to ensure normal progress. As an adult it is easy to forget how difficult it is to learn to spell all words correctly, and so if you find a few errors in your child's work you may immediately jump to the conclusion that his spelling is below average which might be a false assumption. Check first with the child to find out what sort of help they are given at school, then please check with the school to find out whether your child is below standard and also what methods are employed by the teacher.

If you are dissatisfied with the results of your enquiries by all means help your child *but* do not make the child feel he is some sort of failure or is being punished for not achieving your expectations. A child soon rebels when a parent tries to assume the role of the teacher, so make sure that your help is real help offered for genuine reasons, and that the activities you devise are casual and as unlike school tasks as possible.

One of the easiest ways of helping your child is to devise activities which will assist with learning the words for the weekly spelling tests. The photograph game described on page 68 is a simple one which not only tests the child but gives him an opportunity to tell you how he remembered different chunks in the word. As mentioned in the description of the game, please do not try to tell him how to divide the word. He has to develop his own strategies which work for him and if you show real interest in his strategies he will gain confidence in his own ability.

If you possess a typewriter this is another way of encouraging a child to learn set words. Leave him alone to type out each word at a time for as many times as he wishes until he feels that he can type the word without looking at the word on the list. When you are trying to type it is very disconcerting having somebody watching your every move – although it is fascinating to watch – hence the insistence upon leaving the child alone while he types. Also many children do not like others to know their difficulties, so are happiest learning on their own.

Why does typing help? The reasons are many and varied but some can be summarised as follows:

1. The typewriter gives a clear reproduction of the word.
2. It can be operated more quickly than writing in longhand.
3. It operates in the correct left to right direction.
4. It forces the learner to reproduce each letter in its correct order, for insertion later is a most difficult thing to achieve.
5. In order to achieve the goal of typing the word without looking at the word on the list, the learner has to hold an image of the word in his memory for as long as it takes him to type all the letters. This is not easy for the learner but shows him the necessity of forming an image, especially with long words.
6. Each letter is of equal importance.
7. Visual perception of a word is rapid and the image is sometimes hazy, but by typing the word the process is slowed down and each letter is noted.
8. Most children find typing fun especially as the results look grown-up.

Common Words

If the common words are the stumbling block, then test him on these words, allowing him to mark his own, and make sure you show genuine praise for the number of words he *can* spell. It is most important that he gains confidence in his ability to spell at least some of the most frequently used words. If he appreciates that he already knows most of the ordinary words he needs for writing, then he will not be outfaced by the writing task provided he keeps it simple. Let him compose short sentences using the words he knows how to spell. These can then be used for short dictation practice and will most likely show him that he isn't as bad as he thought he was. Chapter Eight contains lists of some of the most common words.

The common words he finds difficult can be taught by way of word bingo which can be made simply at home by the learner himself. On plain postcards draw some boxes, not too many, and leave spaces between so that the words stand out clearly. The learner can select the words himself and either write or type the words into a set number of boxes. He must also make small cards containing these words for 'calling out'. Now all that is needed are some small pieces of coloured paper or card to cover up the words once they have been called.

The learner may not wish to play with you since you are a grown-up, or even more important his parent whom he wishes to impress rather than show his failure. However, do try to explain that this is only a game of chance, not one where the skilled player wins. It all depends upon which words are called out first and he is just as likely to win, or lose, as anyone else. However, the game can be played with other members of the family or even Action Men or imaginary friends. Under these circumstances he will have to call out all the cards but he can still have a card of his own if he wishes. The point of the exercise is to give him plenty of opportunity to study the words, which he does when he scans his card, and it also affords him practice in reading out words in isolation. It is not quite clear why reading aloud helps spelling but there does seem to be some indication that this is so.

Resources

All spellers, good and bad, need to check their work and be skilled in using all available sources to make certain that words are spelt correctly. Everyone needs to check a spelling at some time but unfortunately most poor spellers seem oblivious to this fact. They think that everyone else knows every spelling, so if they have to resort to finding out a spelling they are displaying their ignorance.

Although the dictionary is one source of correct spelling it does not provide all words, and moreover it is not a source which even the most skilled writer invariably uses. The child should be encouraged to think first, 'Where can I find the correct spelling in the shortest possible time?'

First let us consider names, which probably cause the most personal insult if they are spelt incorrectly. If the child is uncertain how his friends spell their names, the most obvious thing is to ask them, especially if the work is being done at school and they are sitting close by. Again, with an address it is safest to ask for the correct spelling of roads and towns; the competent speller would ask, so the poor speller must feel equally justified in asking. A good speller is not afraid to ask for spelling but a poor speller feels embarrassed, so if he can overcome these feelings at least for proper nouns he will achieve a more sane attitude towards spelling and at the same time his work will contain fewer spelling mistakes. Your task here is simply to let him know that it is alright to ask. If he finds that most people say their names or addresses too fast for him, get him to ask them to repeat it more slowly, ask them to write it themselves, or if possible have a go at the word first so that when he asks them for the correct spelling he is merely checking his own efforts.

Sometimes the problem word is obviously to hand, and it is the learner's job to be alert to such possibilities. There is no point worrying over how to spell the name of the month when a calendar is readily available, nor for the child to fret over the word *industrialisation* when a quick look round the room would show him the word on a poster or work card. If the word is a specialised word such as *industrialisation* which relates to their topic work, then the word is most likely to be available somewhere pretty close. Sometimes the word is actually in the question but the child does not think to look back to check. Therefore teach your child to think 'smart'. Even if it does not improve his spelling, at least no-one will know from the finished piece of work that he was unable to spell some of the difficult words. Knowing that he was able to overcome these stumbling blocks on his own will give him confidence to tackle more difficult writing assignments.

Finally, the dictionary is an excellent source of word checking, especially for the good speller, but a yoke for the poor speller. To use a dictionary well one has to have a fairly good idea of the correct spelling in the first place in order to locate the word by the first three

123

letters. Even the first three letters only narrows down the choice and a good impression of the whole word has to be formed before the word can be checked.

However, since this section is merely supplementing normal teaching it is assumed that your particular learner can jot down a rough impression of the word and the task facing him is only to check this word by use of the dictionary. His prime aim is to use the dictionary quickly so that he can write down the correct spelling and then get on with his writing before the flow of thoughts dries up. Speed is very important.

Dictionary games devised to encourage speed in word location are to be found in Chapter Seven. The parent can easily adapt these activities for use at home and since the child can work on his own, the parent can stay in the background.

Throughout all this work it is important that the parent does not intrude too much into the learning situation. Encourage the child to play word games and try the activities suggested, which will probably help him to improve his spelling. You are in the position of *helping*, not tutoring.

Possibly the most important thing that the parent can do for the child is to show a genuine interest in his progress. Show concern for what he *can* do, rather than what he can't. If you, yourself, had difficulty with spelling there is every chance that your child will eventually be a competent speller for you will not expect too much from him and you will show real pleasure in his achievements, however small. Knowing that his parent has confidence in him goes a long way towards creating self-confidence in the child.

Poor spellers have very low self-esteem in relation to spelling. They are highly sensitive to their failure, and so please tread warily.

Remedial Teaching

What is meant by the child in need of remedial teaching? Unfortunately there is no easy answer to this question with regard to spelling, for there is no reliable test which will indicate whether a child is definitely below standard. This means that it is very much left to the teacher to discover which children need extra help with spelling. This is no easy matter, since we do not know what to expect from all ten year olds for example. This results in the strange circumstances where a child from one school is given special help with spelling and in another school the same child would be considered about average for his age group.

Therefore, should your child be receiving remedial spelling lessons there is no need to be alarmed that he is in some way a failure. It simply means that the school considers your child needs help with spelling in order to reach the standard of his classmates in that particular school. For goodness sake do not make him feel that he is a scholastic failure even though you may find many misspellings in his work. As an adult, it is difficult to recall how long it takes to master spelling, and misspellings are quite common even among well-educated adults.

Often a child requires extra help with many aspects of English besides spelling, such as language and reading. However, it is not unusual to find an intelligent child who is able to cope with all the other subjects, failing miserably at spelling, and this spelling difficulty unfortunately affects all his written work. Such a child usually feels his inadequacy very deeply, especially as his worth in other subjects is downgraded by his failure to master spelling.

This is possibly the most difficult position for the parent. If your child is failing miserably in spelling you are possibly the last person he wants to help him. What he needs from you is (a) a belief in his own worth even though he is an atrocious speller, and (b) a sane attitude towards spelling. Let us consider these two points.

When a person is highly anxious about failing he is more likely to fail. His concentration is at a low level as he continually hears a voice saying, 'I can't do it, I can't do it!' Think of yourself in a stressful situation such as climbing a high cliff, crawling into a pothole, making a speech in front of strangers, or even making a simple mathematical calculation which sends some people into confusion. Instead of concentrating upon the task in hand, your mind dwells only on the panic generated by the situation. Others might think you are not even trying and in a way they are right, for you have not yet reached the position where you are able to try. Panic is a barrier to learning, so the first task is to remove the stressful situation.

A really bad speller feels his failure most keenly but he should be helped to see that spelling is not all-important, there are many more important things in life. A sense of failure assumes gigantic proportions to the child concerned and it is your job to try and calm him down and get it into perspective.

Make sure the child has opportunity to be good at something else which will in some way go towards compensating for failure in spelling. He might be good at sport or be a knowledgeable spectator, he might prove to be a good musician, wonderful at performing magic tricks or just a pleasant, likeable person. However, the spelling problem will not just disappear, so it is wise to take a fresh look at this as well.

If your child is deeply embarrassed about his spelling failure, try to work with the school so that your child receives the most appropriate teaching. If you feel that your child would benefit by less attention to his spelling mistakes in other subjects, please discuss it with the school. If your child is fretting unduly over lists of words to be learnt, then again let the school know. Although teachers try very hard to be in tune with the requirements of the children they teach, this is not always possible with such large numbers. Good teachers always welcome information from parents, especially as some children hide their worries from teachers and instead put on a surly attitude or vacant expression.

The school might also provide you with some guidance in some spelling work which is causing particular problems with your child, such as dictionary work or handwriting. Of course, just because the school has asked for your help this does not mean that you now assume the role of teacher's assistant. As mentioned earlier the main help you can give is of a supportive nature, so resist the temptation to set up a little school in your home, however appealing the image might seem to you.

If your child is willing to let you help him and you receive no guidance from his school, I would suggest you read the chapter on remedial teaching. But if any bad feelings develop between you, drop the whole matter as graciously as possible, and don't let any hard feelings remain just because your child would not be taught by you. This is very common.

With the remedial child it is often best to employ a private tutor for half-hour lessons once a week. By all means discuss it with your child's teacher if you think it best, but in these circumstances be guided by yourself, and most of all by your child. He will, of course, be nervous at his first lesson but within two or three lessons he should have settled down and be enjoying himself. If it still remains a painful experience, ask him if he wishes to stop the lessons, for there is nothing to be gained forcing him from one stressful situation into another. Also I would cancel all lessons if he returned home with a list of spelling rules to learn, for such rules will not help a remedial speller but rather confuse him. What you want is a sympathetic, skilled teacher who makes the lessons fun, interesting and encourages the child to write so that he succeeds. Do not expect miracles at first, for the teacher will be trying to build up the child's confidence in writing, but with good teaching you will find the child gradually writing more and with this will come a more positive attitude towards spelling.

Finally, remember Rabbit's words in *The House at Pooh Corner*: Christopher Robin respects Owl, because you can't help respecting anybody who can spell TUESDAY, even if he doesn't spell it right, but spelling isn't everything. There are days when spelling Tuesday simply doesn't count. (*The House at Pooh Corner* p. 73)

Checklists

Checklist 1

Name _____ Age/Class _____

Letters	a	b	c	d	e	f	g	h	i	j	k	l	m	n	o	p	q	r	s	t	u	v	w	x	y	z
Copied																										
Memorised																										
Named																										
Other forms																										
Capital: written																										
recognised																										

Common words	name	and	I	in	is	it	my	of	the	to	went
Copied											
Memorised											

Other words						
Copied						
Memorised						

Coding system	Letters								Letter pairs				
Has taken part in a 'hunt'													
Can sort into 'sets'													

Attitude to writing:

Checklist 2

Name _____ Age/Class _____

Common words	a	are	at	be	can	for	have	he	his	not	on
Copied											
Memorised											

Common words	said	she	so	that	they	was	we	with	you
Copied									
Memorised									

Useful words									
Copied									
Memorised									

Useful words									
Copied									
Memorised									

Dictation Date:	3 words	4 words	5 words	6 words	more than 6 words

Coding system	Letter groups									
Has taken part in a 'hunt'										
Can sort into 'sets'										

Attitude to writing:

Name _____ Age/Class _____

Common words | | | | | | | | | | | |
Copied | | | | | | | | | | | |
Memorised | | | | | | | | | | | |

Common words | | | | | | | | | | | |
Copied | | | | | | | | | | | |
Memorised | | | | | | | | | | | |

Useful words | | | | | | | | | | | |
Copied | | | | | | | | | | | |
Memorised | | | | | | | | | | | |

Dictation
Date:

___ words	___ words	___ words	more than ___ words

Coding system

Letter groups												

Has taken part in a 'hunt'

Resources: _____

_____

_____

Word building: _____

_____

_____

Bibliography

Bryan, W. L. and Harter, N. (1897) 'Studies on the Telegraphic Language. The Acquisition of a hierarchy of habits.' *Psych. Review*, 6: 345–75
Bullock Report (1975) *A Language for Life*, London: H.M.S.O.
Burt, C. (1947) *Mental and Scholastic Tests*, London: Staples

Chomsky, C. (1971) 'Write First, Read Later', *Childhood Education*, 47, 296–299

Dewey, J. (1938) *Experience and Education*, New York: Macmillan
Diack, H. (1960) *Reading and the Psychology of Perception*, Nottingham: Peter Skinner

Frith, U. (Ed) (1980) *Cognitive Processes in Spelling*, London: Academic Press

Gilbert, L. C. and Gilbert D. W. (1942) 'Training for Speed and Accuracy of Visual Perception in Learning to Spell', *University of Caifornia Publications in Education*, VII, No. 5, 351–426
Gray, W. S. (1960) 'What is involved in word perception' in Melnik A. and Merritt J. (Eds.) *The Reading Curriculum*, London: University of London Press and Open University Press

Hildreth G. (1955) *Teaching Spelling*, New York: Henry Holt
Hildreth G. (1959) *Teaching Reading*, New York: Henry Holt
Horn, E. S. (1960) in Harris C. W. (Ed.) *Encyclopedia of Educational Research*, New York: Macmillan

James W. (1890) *The Principles of Psychology*, New York: Henry Holt
Jensen, A. R. (1962) 'Spelling Errors and the Serial-position Effect', *J. of Ed. Psychol.*, 53, 3, 105–109

Livingston, A. A. (1961) 'A Study of Spelling Errors' in Scottish Council for Research in Education, *Studies in Spelling*, London: University of London Press
Longley, C. (Ed.) (1975) *BBC Adult Literacy Handbook*, London: BBC

MacKay, D. and Simo, J. (1976) *Help Your Child to Read and Write and More*, Harmondsworth: Penguin

MacKay, D., Thompson, B., and Schaub, P. (1978) *Breakthrough to Literacy: Teacher's Manual*, London: Longman

McLeod, M. E. (1961) 'Rules in the Teaching of Spelling' in Scottish Council for Research in Education, *Studies in Spelling*, London: University of London Press

Milne, A. A. *The House at Pooh Corner*, London: Methuen

Peters, M. L. (1967) *Spelling: Caught or Taught?* London: Routledge & Kegan Paul

Peters, M. L. (1979) 'Spelling: Generalisation not Rules', *Special Education*, 5, 19–21

Postman, L. and Bruner, J. S. (1948) 'Perception Under Stress', *Psych. Review*, 55: 314–23

Schonell, F. J. (1942) *Backwardness in the Basic Subjects*, Edinburgh: Oliver & Boyd

Thompson, B. (1970) *Learning to Read. A Guide for Teachers and Parents*, London: Sidgwick & Jackson

Torbe, M. (1978) *Teaching Spelling*, London: Ward Lock

Vernon, M. D. (1962) *The Psychology of Perception*, London: University of London Press

Vernon, P. E. (1963) *Personality Assessment: A Critical Survey*, London: Methuen

Vincent, D. and Cresswell, M. (1976) *Reading Tests in the Classroom*, Slough: National Foundation for Educational Research

Wedell, K. (1973) *Learning and Perceptuo-motor Disabilities in Children*, London: John Wiley

Wight-Boycott, V. (1978) 'Fun and First Aid for Weak Spellers', *Remedial Education*, 13, 2, 100–103

Notes